THE GRAVEDIGGERS

by

Phyllis Schlafly

and

Chester Ward
Rear Admiral, United States Navy (Ret.)

PERE MARQUETTE PRESS

P. O. BOX 316 ALTON, ILLINOIS

None of the information contained in this book is classified; nor was any of it obtained from classified sources. No Government security regulations have been broken — only the "managed news" barrier. All the facts and figures contained herein, and the programs revealed, have been available to Soviet Intelligence through official or public sources. It is no coincidence, however, that the composite picture of these programs has never before been available to the American people.

October 1964

Printed in the United States of America

Table of Contents

"If we desire to secure peace . . . it must be known that we are at all times ready for war."
— GEORGE WASHINGTON
December 3, 1793

"The campaign we launch today is dedicated to peace through preparedness."
— SENATOR BARRY GOLDWATER
September 3, 1964

Chapter One

WHO WILL BURY US?

"In the end . . . a funeral requiem will be sung over the Soviet Republic or over world capitalism."[1]   —LENIN

"History is on our side. We will bury you."[2]
          — KHRUSHCHEV

The Communists always want to bury anything that stands in their way of world conquest. When Khrushchev moved his missiles into Cuba, he taunted us:

"Now the remains of this [Monroe] Doctrine should best be buried, as every dead body is, so that it does not poison the air by its decay."[3]

Why is Khrushchev so confident of burying us, when Lenin thought Communism had only a 50/50 chance? The answer is that Khrushchev has the help of American gravediggers. These men are not Communists. They are card-carrying liberals. They will not commit the crime. They will merely dig the grave.

These gravediggers move in and out of the highest levels of our Government. They are bringing about what our past enemies, King George III, Napoleon, the Kaiser, Hitler and Tojo, could never accomplish. They are proving the famous prophecy of Abraham Lincoln:

5

"All the armies of Europe, Asia and Africa combined, . . . with a Bonaparte for a commander, could not by force take a drink from the Ohio or make a track on the Blue Ridge in a trial of a thousand years. . . . . If destruction is our lot we must ourselves be its author and finisher."[4]

During the Battle of Britain of World War II, Winston Churchill paid an eloquent tribute to the Royal Air Force: "Never in history was so much owed by so many to so few." This book about the gravediggers shows that "Never in history have so few gambled so recklessly with the lives of so many."

Do you know who is digging YOUR grave so that Khrushchev can fulfill his boast?

Do you know who is *really* risking nuclear war?

Chapter Two

THE BIGGEST GYP
IN HISTORY

In 1940 tourists came from far and near to admire the fabulous new Tacoma Narrows Bridge. To make it so beautiful, the engineering tradition which demanded firm and massive strength had been cast aside as an "old myth." The unusual Bridge design with its slender girders was based on the belief that "new realities" of coexistence with storm winds would permit the sacrifice of firmness for flexibility. Survival of the structure was staked on accommodating to pressures, on flexing and giving, rather than firmly resisting the elements. Engineers and motorists alike enjoyed explaining the advantages of the new flexible accommodation design.

To protect its investment, the city of Tacoma, Washington took out a large insurance policy to cover the Bridge. Four months after the Bridge was opened, an unexpected wind came. With each gust the flexible Bridge flexed a little more. Finally the wind caused the deck of the Bridge to bend clear of its supporting cables. The flexible Bridge, which natives had dubbed "Galloping Gertie", plunged into Puget Sound.

Immediate plans were made to rebuild the Bridge with the payment from the insurance com-

panies. Then the awful truth was revealed: One
of the insurance agents had gambled that the
Tacoma Bridge could never fall, and had diverted
the annual premium to his own pocket. When he
had looked at the Bridge with its fortune in modern steel, his bet had looked like a sure road to
easy money. But his gamble failed, and trusting
people discovered too late they did not have the
protection they paid for.

For four years the Kennedy-Johnson Administration has pretended to spend more than 50 percent of the annual Federal budget on defense.
American taxpayers, paying the highest peacetime
taxes in history, think they are buying military
strength and security against our enemies. But
they are victims of the biggest gyp in history. Day
by day in many ways, Robert Strange McNamara
is making us weaker and weaker. We are not
getting the defense protection we are paying for.

Lyndon Johnson and Robert McNamara are
taking two dangerous gambles with the lives of
190,000,000 Americans. Like the Tacoma insurance agent, they are gambling that the United
States will never need the defense protection we
are paying for. Therefore they are diverting funds
from defense muscle — such as the advanced-type
bombers, the aero-space weapons systems, the
Nike-Zeus and Nike-X missile killers. Instead they
are spending vast sums on non-military boon-
doggles such as putting a man on the moon, and
on purely political projects such as the Poverty
Bill.

Also, like the Tacoma Bridge designer, Johnson

and McNamara are gambling that accommodation is better than strength, and that being flexible is safer than being firm. The American people have not been told that their money and their lives have been staked on wishful thinking that the Soviets are "mellowing" and will never attack us. Americans have been kept ignorant of their risk by bureaucratic doubletalk, managed news, and McNamara's myths. Fatal weaknesses in the Kennedy-Johnson foreign policy of "accommodation" have been concealed by inflated boasts of military strength.

Do the American people want to take those gambles?

Twice during the last four years our elected leaders gambled with our safety — and lost.

You would be dead now — if your life had been staked on the Kennedy-Johnson Administration's gamble in 1961 that we could continue to trust the Soviets not to betray the first nuclear test ban. With no prior warning, and in the midst of test-ban talks in Geneva, the Soviets set off a series of multi-megaton bombs many times larger than anything the U. S. has exploded before or since.

You would be dead now — if your life had been staked on the Kennedy-Johnson Administration's gamble in 1962 that it was safe to trust the Soviets not to put "offensive" missiles on Cuba. All the world knows now that the Soviets were doing precisely that *at the very time* the Soviet Ambassador was in the White House promising the contrary to President Kennedy.

In both of these cases, the Administration gambled with the lives and freedom of American citizens. Both gambles resulted in major defeats for the United States.

By trapping us in the test ban, Khrushchev stole our supremacy in nuclear super-weapons — and thereby gained the *power* necessary to destroy us. In the Cuban crisis, he gained the *knowledge* necessary to destroy us. Here is what he learned:

1) Khrushchev confirmed what he had told Robert Frost a few months before: Americans are "too liberal to fight" — you "will sit on one hand and then on the other — even when your vital interests are involved!"[1] He learned that the present U. S. leadership will not even take the steps necessary to defend America against Soviet missiles in Cuba ready to destroy millions of Americans on a moment's notice.

2) Khrushchev learned there is no penalty for betraying his promises to the U. S., and no penalty for threatening us with first-strike weapons inside our radar screen.

3) Khrushchev learned that he did not need to spend billions to harden expensive missile sites to withstand a U. S. defensive strike — because there would never be any such strike; so he could safely put the same money into "soft" missiles, suitable for a surprise attack against the United States, and get five times as much firepower.

Now the same leaders — who twice gambled with our safety and lost — are staking American lives in the greatest gamble since the dawn of civilization. Like the insurance agent who gambled that the Bridge would never fall, they are gambling that the Soviets will never attack. They are betting that Khrushchev didn't mean it when he said "we will bury you." They are gambling that the Communists, after successfully conquering one billion people, will about-face and abandon their goal of world conquest.

It is on this gamble that the Johnson Administration is failing to give us the defense we need, the defense we are paying for, the defense which can give us peace *without* surrender.

Your life and the lives of your children are staked on this gamble. The biggest gyp in history has laid our freedom and independence on the line. Time is running out. If our choice is wrong in 1964 — there will be no second chance.

Chapter Three

THE McNAMARA GAP

In 1960 the Kennedy-Johnson team made a major campaign issue out of the "missile gap" which they alleged to be the fault of the Eisenhower Administration. This "missile gap" was nothing but a mere future possibility, which was exploited as if it were real by New Frontier ghostwriters. Immediately after the election, the Defense Department admitted that it had never actually developed.

Four years later the American people are faced with what can be accurately described as the "McNamara gap." Secretary of Defense Robert McNamara has created so many gaps in our military strength that his defense failures exceed even his previous failure with the Edsel automobile.

Here is the defense the American people have paid for but are NOT getting under the policies of Robert Strange McNamara:[1]

ON THE LAND

Missile Bases in Turkey, Italy and England. Our bases in Turkey and Italy, capable of firing 45 Jupiter nuclear missiles deep into the USSR, were dismantled within weeks after the 1962 Cuban crisis by the Kennedy-Johnson Administration as part of the "deal"[2] with Khrushchev. Four Thor missile bases in England with 60 nuclear missiles capable of striking Soviet targets have been dismantled. These two missile programs represented a U. S. defense investment of many hundreds of millions of dollars — thrown away to accommodate Khrushchev.

Bomber Bases in England, Spain, Morocco, Libya and Guam. These giant U. S. Air Force bases equipped for nuclear bombers are now being closed down. We are retreating from the atomic deterrent ring we had placed around the Soviet Union.

Atomic Weapons. By the orders of President Kennedy in February 1961 and President Johnson in January and April 1964, the production of nuclear materials for military purposes was cut about 50 percent.[3] Defense appropriations in the last two years have already cut by 40 percent the procurement of *strategic* nuclear weapons — the only type which can deter the Soviets from launching a surprise attack against the U. S.

Mobile Missile Bases. The plan to have our intercontinental Minuteman missiles on mobile launching sites such as railroad cars, so as to be safe from enemy first-strike attack, was vetoed by McNamara. The only Minuteman missiles he is buying are vulnerable to the much more powerful Soviet missiles.

Mobile Medium Range Ballistic Missile. This nuclear-tipped weapon, to be fired from a truck with a range of 1,000 miles, was cited by McNamara in April, 1964, as a new weapons project. He cancelled it in August, 1964, after $100 million was spent on its development.[4]

Bacteriological and Chemical Weapons Systems. "Future war," Marshal Zhukov told the 20th Communist Party Conference in Moscow, "will be characterized by atomic, thermonuclear, chemical and bacteriological weapons." Rear Admiral Cecil Coggins, M.D., former Chief of Atomic Bacteriological and Chemical Warfare for the U. S. Navy, charged:

> "We have neglected to develop an offensive capability in chemical war and have no defense worthy of the name. . . . In biological warfare . . . we have neither an offensive nor a defensive capability."[5]

IN THE AIR

Nike-Zeus Missile Killer. Development for production of this remarkable anti-missile-missile, which scored four direct hits on incoming missiles in successful tests,[6] was cancelled by McNamara.

Skybolt Missile. This missile which would enable bombers to hit targets deep inside Russia, without flying over Soviet soil or within range of Soviet anti-aircraft, was cancelled by McNamara. It would have kept the nearly 700 U. S. SAC heavy bombers — which carry 90 percent of U. S. strategic striking power — effective against Soviet air defense for another 5 to 10 years.

B-70 Super Bomber. McNamara halted development for production of this bomber designed to carry heavy nuclear weapons at triple-sonic speeds deep into the USSR.

B-58, B-52 and B-47 Bombers. All production has been stopped on these bombers which are the backbone of our Strategic Air Command. Not a single new bomber has been built for the U. S. since 1962. For the first time in 25 years, no U. S. bombers are under development or construction. The B-47s are scheduled to be placed on the "bomber bonfire" Dean Rusk is offering to Khrushchev. Even if the Soviets burn none of theirs, McNamara will scrap or "deactivate" all of ours — just as he has already scrapped the B-47 bases that formerly ringed Soviet Russia. All production lines for the B-52's — our most powerful weapons system of any type — were closed down during the Cuban missiles crisis of 1962, and have never been reopened. Although Congress appropriated $525 million for another wing of B-52s, McNamara refused to spend what Congress considered essential for U. S. security.

Atlas Missile. 129 of these missiles produced at a cost of $5.4 billion are being scrapped by McNamara. The Atlas Missile can carry nuclear warheads six to eight times more powerful than the Minuteman which McNamara tells us will replace it.

AMPSS. This is the Advanced Manned Precision Strike System badly wanted by our Air Force. It has been blocked by McNamara.

Pluto Missile. Described as the "most powerful single weapon yet conceived," this atomic-propelled missile carries a nuclear warhead, flies at 2,000 miles an hour, too low to be picked up by enemy radar, and has a round-the-world range. It was cancelled by McNamara's orders — after an outlay of $200 million.[7]

Dyna-Soar Orbital Bomber. Designed by Boe-

ing to carry nuclear weapons in orbit, this proto-
type was cancelled by Lyndon Johnson 10 days
after he became President, although $400 million
had been spent on its development.

ON THE SEA

Aircraft Carriers. Our 15 attack aircraft carriers
are being stripped by McNamara of their strategic
nuclear bombers.[8] Known in the Navy as "heavy
attack aircraft", these planes can carry hydrogen
bombs up to 4,000,000 times more powerful than
the conventional bombs which the new "light attack aircraft" replacing them are designed to carry.
Under the McNamara schedule, the last of these
15 most powerful warships in the world will be
withdrawn from "strategic alert" mission in the
fiscal year beginning in 1965. This will destroy
one of our most reliable deterrents against Soviet
nuclear surprise attack on the United States —
because the Soviets could not destroy these ships
with their ICBMs. Such an attack could not be
deterred by reliance on small tactical nuclear
weapons.

Polaris Surface Ships. Surface ships can be
armed with 10 to 16 Polaris missiles each, and are
much cheaper and faster to build than nuclear
submarines. The administration will largely fi-
nance them for NATO — but not for the U. S.
They would greatly strengthen our deterrent. If
they are so good for NATO, and are needed, why
does McNamara refuse them to us?

Typhoon Missile Ships. This new weapons system would give the U. S. Navy mobile missile

"bases", which could move in as close to Russia as necessary, to protect all elements of U. S. seapower (aircraft carriers, cruisers, destroyers, etc.) against Soviet air and air-to-ground missile attack. It was cancelled by McNamara.

Retreat from the Mediterranean. By closing down our missile launching sites and bomber bases in Italy, Turkey, Northern Africa and Spain, and by not acquiring any new missile sites, McNamara is surrendering control of the Mediterranean which leads to the soft underbelly of Russia. Now the Soviets have missile sites close to us in Cuba, but we have none close to Russia. Hitler did not dare go to war as long as control of the Czechoslovakian flank deep in Germany's side was in unfriendly hands. As long as we had many strategic nuclear weapons in the Mediterranean area, only a few minutes away from Soviet targets, Soviet strategists would not approve a strike at U. S. targets on the other side of the globe.

❉   ❉   ❉   ❉

While cancelling all these weapons which are effective and necessary to our defense, McNamara has not authorized or developed a single new strategic weapons system. Maintaining our national defense requires new weapons to replace what is obsolete. France lost heavily at the start of World Wars I and II because its soldiers were equipped with only weapons of the previous war.

The McNamara gap also results from weaker warhead power — less megatonnage — in our missiles. Warhead power depends upon the yield/weight ratio and the warhead weight which the missile's rocket thrust can deliver. The Joint Chiefs concede that the Soviets are ahead in these fields.

Our intercontinental ballistic missiles now probably average only a fraction more than 2 megatons of explosive power: theirs, between 13 and 30 megatons. Taking McNamara's own latest figures[9] on ICBMs, our number — 800 — times 2 megatons plus 256 Polaris times 1 megaton=1856 megatons. Taking McNamara's low estimated Soviet number — 200 times 21½ megatons (average)=4,300 megatons. This would give the Soviets a net missile-explosive-power-gap of more than 2400 megatons — that is, 2 billion, 400 million *tons* of TNT equivalent.

Thus, using McNamara's own numbers of missiles, the Soviet missiles already could carry more than twice the explosive power of the total of U. S. missiles. This gap will widen with extreme rapidity in the near future as the U. S. phases out its liquid-fueled Atlas and Titan I missiles which carry 5 or 10 megatons, and instead concentrates production on the much smaller 1-megaton Minuteman. The consensus of estimates of future U. S. missile power is based on a warhead average of 1 megaton.

McNamara plans a total U. S. missile force by 1966 of 1,000 Minuteman, 656 Polaris, and 54 Titan II. The explosive power in the total of their warheads would equal about 2,200 megatons. Within the last year, the Soviets have doubled their warhead explosive power. If they should build only one-fourth as many missiles, as the U. S., the new explosive power of their warheads (then averaging 30 MT) would total about 12,800 megatons. The explosive-power or McNamara gap in their favor would then amount to some 10,600 megatons, or 10 billion, 600 million tons of TNT.

When all the pieces are put together, the Mc-Namara gap presents a pattern of unilateral disarmament that one does not have to be a military expert to see. It looks as though the gravediggers are determined to lose the nuclear arms race, just as they lost the Bay of Pigs invasion and are losing South Viet Nam.

Khrushchev is already exploiting for purposes of nuclear blackmail the new favorable balance of strategic power which U. S. unilateral nuclear disarmament is giving him. The public has heard little about it because "managed news" tells us that his reaction to U. S. retaliation against North Viet Nam in the Gulf of Tonkin was "mild." Actually, on August 8, 1964 he again bellowed that he would bury us, saying:

> "If the imperialists dare to unleash war, this
> war . . . will result in the full destruction of
> capitalism."

Almost immediately after the Khrushchev threat, Deputy Secretary of Defense Cyrus Vance "quietly removed the naval patrols from the Gulf of Tonkin." This type of Soviet nuclear threat — and prompt U. S. retreat — foreshadows the future for an America disarmed down to second-best to the USSR. As forcefully stated by General Maxwell D. Taylor, former Chairman of the Joint Chiefs of Staff: "There will be no living long with Communism as an inferior."

Chapter Four

OUR ENEMY'S SECRET WEAPON

At the end of World War II, the United States was the most powerful nation in all history. Our scientists and engineers had perfected most of the important weapons of World War II. Our soldiers had captured the best German missile designs, and scientists such as Dr. Werner Von Braun.

In 1945 the Soviet Union was a devastated nation, pulled through to victory only by $11 billion of American lend-lease aid. The Communists had failed to develop even one new military weapon since they seized power in 1917. But the Soviets had an objective, a plan, and the determination to reach their goal. They laid out their blueprint for world conquest as clearly as did Hitler in *Mein Kampf*. The Communists worked to fulfill Lenin's famous prophecy:

> "As long as capitalism remains we cannot live in peace. In the end one or the other will triumph."[1]

How could this third-rate power, which had difficulty defeating little Finland, hope to compete with the United States of America? Obviously, it didn't have a chance, militarily or economically. There was only one field in which the Communists clearly outdistanced Americans — in psychological warfare. Soviet strategists were greatly influenced by what the legendary Chinese strategist Sun Tzu wrote in *The Art of War* about 500 B.C.:

> "To fight and conquer in all your battles is not supreme excellence; supreme excellence consists in breaking the enemy's resistance without fighting."

The Soviets developed a new strategy of conquest by psychological warfare — so good that it represents the only really great advance in 2,500 years. In Sun Tzu's version, the aggressor, although conserving his resources by not fighting, still had to expend energy to "break" the victim's resistance. The Soviet strategists went far beyond Sun Tzu and developed a "super-supreme excellence" — which consists of manipulating U. S. leadership into destroying our own resistance.

Thus the Communists have made the defeat of the United States a "do it yourself" project for Americans. To discover ways and means of accomplishing this, and to train the Soviet experts needed, the Communists founded the Lenin School of Political Warfare in Moscow, the Far Eastern University in Peiping, and the psychological warfare schools in Prague.

Graduates of these word-warfare schools became skilled practitioners of the Communist technique called "opinion subversion". J. Edgar Hoover was the first to expose this prime weapon of Soviet conquest. He defined it as the Red attempt "to influence American opinion." Mr. Hoover described how "the process of opinion subversion is developed with such diabolical skill that even today a surprising number of victims are drawn into the active promotion of causes which advance Communist aims and ideas."[2]

By means of the "super-supreme" weapon of "opinion subversion," the Reds set out to induce Americans: (1) *not* to safeguard our atomic and hydrogen secrets, (2) *not* to develop the weapons we need to retain our military supremacy, (3) *not* to produce the weapons we have already developed, and (4) *not* to use the weapons we have.

Let us see how successful were the Soviet strategists in influencing American opinion.

THE ATOM BOMB

In the 1940s the Communists made their greatest scientific gains by the recruitment of little-known agents who collected big secrets, such as Julius and Ethel Rosenberg, Harry Gold, David Greenglass and Morten Sobell, all of whom were convicted in well-publicized trials;[3] and scientists who escaped behind the Iron Curtain, such as Dr. Bruno Pontecorvo,[4] Dr. Peter Kapitza[5] and Dr. Joan Hinton.[6] While espionage and defection are still a major Communist effort, the Reds began as early as World War II to shift their emphasis to the direct influence of American policy.

First the Reds convinced the Roosevelt and Truman administrations that we did not need to protect our atomic secrets against the Communists. Six scientists and one machinist cleared for secret atomic work had been Communists, namely, Klaus Fuchs,[7] David Hawkins,[8] Robert R. Davis,[9] Frank Oppenheimer,[10] Philip Morrison,[11] Alan

Nunn May,[12] and David Greenglass.[13] Fuchs, May and Greenglass were found guilty of stealing our atomic secrets and giving them to Soviet agents. Dr. Sanford Simons walked off with some plutonium, the stuff atom bombs are made of, and his theft was not discovered until four years later.[14]

Arthur Alexandrovich Adams, the master Soviet spy who organized atomic espionage in the United States, was never arrested, although highly-secret information about the Oak Ridge, Tennessee atomic plant was found in his room in New York City in 1944. He was finally permitted to return to Russia with his secrets.[15]

Most of our knowledge of Soviet atomic espionage is based on the files which Igor Gouzenko, the Soviet code clerk, took with him when he fled from the Russian Embassy in Ottawa in September, 1945. In his article *Stalin Sent Me to Spy School,* Gouzenko tells of asking his "section chief" in Moscow "how it was that American and English authorities were unable to uncover our agents when there were so many of them?" His section chief replied:

> "Our strength is in those very numbers. The authorities nip one and think they have 'cleared up the situation' — but nine stay free to continue our work. Moreover, some of our most valued agents are in such high places that they could scarcely be suspected of treason."[16]

Secondly the Reds cultivated prominent dupes who urged that the United States give our atomic secrets to the Soviets even faster than their spies could steal them.

After conferring with Ambassador to Russia
Averell Harriman, Secretary of War Henry L.
Stimson wrote to President Truman in September
of 1945 that he favored sharing "the atomic weapon" with Russia.[17] In 1946 Dean Acheson and
David Lilienthal presented a State Department
plan which called for the building of atomic bomb
plants in other countries including Russia, so that
they "can develop a greater sense of security" and
"a balance will have been established."[18] Senator
Robert Taft described this plan as "the limit of all
asininity on our part."[19]

Then Philip Jessup, whom the Senate later refused to confirm as U. S. Ambassador because of
his far left activities, who is now the U. S. representative on the World Court, wrote a letter de-
manding that we "stop the production of [atomic]
bombs."[20] Shortly after its publication, all manu-
facturing of atomic bombs stopped.[21]

As a result of these gravediggers' activities, the
United States had no sure-fire A-bombs in 1948.
This was the year the Communists began their
Berlin blockade and completed their conquest of
China in confidence that they would not be
stopped by U. S. A-bomb strength.

What did the Soviets gain through years of effort
by Soviet spies and American traitors? Although
they benefited by billions of dollars worth of stolen
scientific techniques and industrial processes, their
greatest gain was time. They needed atomic
powers of destruction, as psychological levers in
their campaign to frighten U. S. gravediggers into

bringing about U. S. nuclear disarmament in order to meet the Soviet timetable for world conquest. How much time did they gain? As stated in a brilliant study recently published on the subject of Soviet atomic espionage:

> "In 1951 the Joint Congressional Atomic Energy Committee was ready to concede that had the Soviets started from scratch, it might have extended the 'nuclear gap' by up to ten years. Other experts set the figure higher."[22]

THE HYDROGEN BOMB

The next significant victory of the Communists, accomplished when few Americans knew what was happening, was to stop U. S. H-bomb development. The theory of the hydrogen bomb was far advanced in 1945, and the bomb could have been ready in 1947. Assistant Secretary of the Army John J. McCloy admitted in December 1946:

> "I have been told by scientists who are not mere theorists but who actually planned and made the bomb which was exploded in New Mexico . . . we were within two years at the close of the war of producing a bomb of the hydrogen-helium type, i.e., a bomb of approximately one thousand times the power of the present bombs."[23]

This slow-down brought about by the gravediggers was so successful that, whereas we had been 4 years ahead in exploding an A-bomb, we were only 1 year ahead on the H-bomb. In 1954 the Atomic Energy Commission revoked J. Robert Oppenheimer's security clearance. The Executive Director of the Congressional Joint Committee on

Atomic Energy, William L. Borden, made a summary of the evidence against Oppenheimer which said in part:

> "He was contributing substantial monthly sums to the Communist Party; . . . he had been instrumental in securing recruits for the Communist Party; and he was in frequent contact with Soviet espionage agents. . . . He was responsible for employing a number of Communists . . . at war-time Los Alamos; . . . He was an enthusiastic sponsor of the A-bomb program until the war ended, when he immediately and outspokenly advocated that the Los Alamos Laboratory be disbanded. . . . He was remarkably instrumental in influencing the military authorities and the Atomic Energy Commission essentially to suspend H-bomb development from mid-1946 through Jan. 31, 1950; he has worked tirelessly, from Jan. 31, 1950 onward, to retard the United States H-bomb program; he has used his potent influence against every post-war effort to expand capacity for producing A-bomb material."[24]

This is the same J. Robert Oppenheimer who, on December 2, 1963, was invited to the White House by Lyndon Johnson and presented with the Enrico Fermi Award. This highest honor conferred by the Atomic Energy Commission carries with it a tax-free purse of $50,000.

THE KOREAN WAR

The next important achievement of the Communist effort to break American resistance was inducing us to abandon victory in the Korean War.

Our commanding officer during the Korean War, General Mark Clark, stated when he signed the truce agreement in Korea:

> "I gained the unenviable distinction of being the first United States Army Commander in history to sign an armistice without a victory."

Was the reason for this that we were held at bay by an enemy with superior military force? Obviously not. We had almost total supremacy in the air, on the sea and in nuclear weapons. Our enemy was a military nonentity, had never beaten any country in war, and had a supply line totally inadequate for combat.

Why then did we not win a clear victory? Because the Kremlin rushed up a battalion of psychological strategists who saved the day for the Reds. While we fired bullets in Korea, the Communists fired a slogan in Washington more potent than the atom bomb. It was: "We mustn't start World War III." This slogan intimidated our Government to such an extent that we refused to use the many weapons we had, such as (1) bombing the Yalu River bridges over which the Reds were pouring to kill American boys, (2) using atomic bombs along the Yalu River, as advocated by General MacArthur, to seal off the battlefield from enemy reinforcements, (3) bombing key military targets within North Korea (such as the Chosen River hydroelectric power plant and the railroad center of Rashin), (4) hot pursuit of enemy planes across the Yalu, and (5) a naval blockade to stop the gasoline and arms coming from Europe. What good did it do to have military supremacy if we didn't have the will to win?

THE FIRST NUCLEAR TEST BAN

In the late 1950s, in spite of the tremendous successes of Soviet atomic espionage agents, in spite of the kidnapping of hundreds of German scientists and making the American Army surrender the great German underground missile factory at Nordhausen with all its advanced designs and pilot models,[25] in spite of our slowdown in the development of the H-bomb, in spite of the Korean War, America still had a commanding two-to-one lead across the entire spectrum of the technology of nuclear weapons. How, then, could Khrushchev fulfill his wish to "bury" us?

The Soviet psychological warfare experts conceived a bold plan to accomplish what Soviet scientists and military men were unable to do. They decided to trick the United States into stopping all nuclear development, while the Soviets secretly raced ahead. This is exactly what happened. In the fall of 1958 Khrushchev successfully induced the United States to adopt a nuclear test moratorium — while undercover, the Soviets pushed full speed ahead.

This significant success of Soviet propaganda was accomplished in spite of the fact that informed Americans warned in advance of the danger. In July 1958, months before the nuclear test moratorium went into effect, the famous report of the American Bar Association Committee on Communist Tactics, Strategy and Objectives called attention to the drive to halt nuclear tests as one of the eleven major current Communist tactics.

The nuclear test moratorium was accomplished over the vigorous protests of such eminent men as the father of the H-bomb, Dr. Edward Teller; the developer of the A-bomb, Dr. Arthur H. Compton; and Atomic Energy Commission Chairmen Lewis L. Strauss and John A. McCone.

Many other capable and patriotic scientists warned against the test ban moratorium. Former U. S. Atomic Energy Commissioner Thomas E. Murray said that the test ban enabled the Soviet Union "to gain a position of decisive advantage in nuclear weapons." He pointed out that this policy has utterly failed to gain us any political or military objective, has seriously endangered our national security, and has left us sitting behind a Maginot Line of obsolescent nuclear weapons while the Soviets have continued to develop and test new weapons and to close the nuclear gap.

Khrushchev's boastful nature made it hard for him to keep the secret of his cheating. On January 14, 1960 he reported to the Deputies of the Russian Communist Party:

> "The Central Committee of the Communist Party and the Soviet Government can inform you, Comrade Deputies, that the weapons we have now are formidable ones, but what is hatching, so to speak, is still more perfect, still more formidable. The weapon that is being developed and is, as they say, in the portfolio of our scientists and designers is an incredible weapon."

In September, 1961, the Soviets abruptly terminated the nuclear test ban talks at Geneva which had been going on for two years, and began the largest series of nuclear tests in history. Khrushchev cheated "big", and ultimately exploded more than 90 bombs, including the largest bomb explosions in history.

It takes at least six months to prepare for one of these large explosions. This series proved that the Soviets had been cheating during the moratorium, that the negotiations at Geneva were a farce and a trap, and that in the area of strategic nuclear warheads, the Soviets had now achieved at least a two-to-one lead over America in the technology of super weapons.

One day in Geneva an enterprising reporter stopped the chief Soviet negotiator, Tsarapkin, and asked him why the Soviet Union broke off the talks in Geneva and exploded a series of nuclear tests. Tsarapkin answered quickly, "Because we had more than a hundred talks and we finally had enough." The reporter asked, "You mean enough talks?" Tsarapkin looked at him coldly and replied, "No, enough bombs." In other words, the negotiations in Geneva were simply a cover for the Soviet effort to surpass America by secretly testing nuclear weapons.

The result of the 3-year nuclear test moratorium was that the Soviets developed the strategic nuclear power that enables Khrushchev to threaten the destruction of the United States. We lost our superiority because our leaders believed Soviet promises. Soviet military experts now brag that the Soviet Union "used its nuclear rocket might to shield Socialist Cuba."

Chapter Five

SUCKERS FOR SLOGANS

How were the Communists able to persuade America to stop the development and production of the weapons we need for our own defense, and to persuade us not to use and to scrap the weapons we already have? This was done by a psychological warfare campaign cleverly designed to appeal to all groups of Americans. Harvard University Professor Henry A. Kissinger, nuclear-strategist consultant to the Eisenhower and the Kennedy-Johnson Administrations, described the Soviet psychological campaign this way:

> "The Communist campaign, finely attuned to prevailing fears, almost imperceptibly shifted the primary concern away from Soviet aggression — the real security problem — to the immorality of the use of nuclear weapons, which happened to be the most effective way of resisting it. Because of its skill in exploiting the inhibitions of the non-Soviet world, the Soviet Union has discovered two forms of 'atomic blackmail': The threat of its growing nuclear arsenal and an appeal to the West's moral inhibitions. In either case, the consequence is a lowered will to resist."[1]

Many Americans are suckers for slogans. Slogans influence our thinking and our buying. Likewise, slogans are Communism's best gimmick.

The Reds have used made-in-Moscow slogans to sell the American people on disarmament. Unlike imported commercial goods, they bear no stamp to betray their alien origin. Yet they are injected into our communications system by Soviet agents and their dupes to poison our pipelines of information.

Ever since the success of Lenin's slogan, "Peace, land, bread," in capturing Russia, the Communists have found slogans a useful weapon. Beginning in 1931 the Communists have achieved amazing success with their use of slogans designed to dupe prominent people.

Millions of people are behind the Iron Curtain today because our leaders were brainwashed with the false slogan that "Russia is a peace-loving democracy." This myth was peddled by such prominent people as Vice President Henry Wallace and Ambassador to Russia Joseph Davies, who reported to Americans:

> "Stalin . . . is decent and clean-living . . . kindly and gentle. A child would like to sit in his lap and a dog would sidle up to him. . . . It is bad Christianity, bad sportsmanship, bad sense to challenge the integrity of the Soviet government."[2]

Such delusions led directly to the tragic agreements of Teheran, Yalta and Potsdam.

Millions of people are behind the Bamboo Curtain today because our State Department accepted the Red slogan that "The Chinese Reds are just agrarian reformers." Hypodermics of this Communist poison were injected into our pipelines of information by such strategically-placed fellow travelers as Owen Lattimore of the State Department, who urged that we let China fall to the Communists, but not "let it look as though we pushed it"; by Edgar Snow who wrote 61 articles for the *Saturday Evening Post*; and by book reviewers for the *New York Times,* who invariably gave favorable reviews to books which peddled the "agrarian reformer" line.

Cuba is under the Communist heel today because Americans were duped by propaganda to make Castro appear as a Robin Hood. This myth was spread by such leading opinion makers as the *New York Times* which told us that Castro was the "Abraham Lincoln of Cuba," and by a leading television personality who said that Castro was the "George Washington of Cuba."

It was the slogan "Capture the national redoubt in the Bavarian Alps" which diverted one American Army from beating the Russians to Berlin, and diverted General Patton's Army from beating the Russians to Prague and Budapest.[3] It was the slogan "Bring the boys home" and Communist-inspired GI riots in Germany and the Philippines that brought about the unilateral dismantling of our military forces at the end of World War II, while the Soviets remobilized and re-armed.

It was the slogan "We mustn't start World War III" which kept America from winning the Korean War or from giving any aid to the Hungarian Freedom Fighters in 1956. We can't invoke the Monroe Doctrine today in order to remove Communist bases in Cuba because that might "start

World War III." We should recognize this slogan as a form of international blackmail practiced on us by the Soviet sloganeers.

By the late 1950s the Communists concentrated their main push on the slogans "peace" and "peaceful coexistence". In a report entitled *The Communist Peace Offensive: A Campaign to Disarm and Defeat the United States,* the U. S. House Committee on Un-American Activities called this propaganda "The most dangerous hoax ever devised by the international Communist conspiracy."

The Soviet sloganeers have become so proficient in their special calling that they have refined very sophisticated versions of the "peace" propaganda, tailormade for particular segments of the American people.

RATHER RED THAN DEAD

In 1958 Lord Bertrand Russell, prominent British Socialist and pacifist, the author of the book arrogantly entitled *Why I Am Not A Christian,* openly advocated surrender to the Communists. He said that we should negotiate with the Soviets but we should let them know in advance that, if we do not reach an agreement, the West will surrender rather than risk nuclear war. This launched the phrase "rather Red than dead," the slogan designed to appeal to the extreme leftists, to pacifists, to scientists, and to eggheads.

In January 1961, Khrushchev directed the Communist Parties of the world to exploit the pacifist circles of the bourgeoise to "mobilize the peoples" to pressure imperialist governments for disarmament.[4] By 1962 peacemongering in the form of dramatizations on the local level appeared in most of the larger American cities. In early February the Reds promoted the first in a series of "General Strikes for Peace." Chapters of the Committee for a Sane Nuclear Policy and the Student Peace Union sponsored pacifist parades with pickets carrying placards urging "Ban the Bomb" and "NO to ALL tests."

In March women from 10 nations paraded in Geneva where the disarmament conference was in session to demand an end to all nuclear tests. The 50 Americans in this pacifist parade cabled President Kennedy asking him to let them take over a U. S. military base near the Soviet Union so they could disarm it and turn it into a cultural exchange center. The turning over of a U. S. military base near the Soviet Union to 50 women pacifists would be as futile as the Children's Crusade of the 13th Century. During the spring, the sidewalk in front of the White House was the scene of many peace pickets, including college students, Professor Linus Pauling and Mrs. Cyrus Eaton.

In April 1962, while Americans celebrated the great feast of Easter, the Communists sponsored "Easter Peace Walks" to sell their poisonous propaganda. In Detroit 1,000 "peace marchers" converged in the center of the city and marched six abreast to Ford Auditorium for a mass rally. In New York the traditional Easter Parade included 5,000 pacifist demonstrators. At the Seattle World's Fair, the local affiliate of "Turn Toward Peace" released 1,000 "peace balloons." In Philadelphia 600 "peace walkers" marched to Independence Hall for a disarmament rally. In Buffalo the Easter Peace Walk was preceded by a 28-hour "peace vigil." In Chicago 2,000 marchers celebrated the end of a week of "peace" agitation. In Boston 2,000 pacifist paraders held a rally at the Boston Common.[5]

This mass agitation was designed to make the disarmament propaganda spread by the gravediggers in the State Department and the Pentagon look downright reasonable and middle-of-the-road.

NUCLEAR WAR IS UNTHINKABLE

The second wave of disarmament propaganda was designed to appeal to the average middle-class American who loves his family, goes to the movies and watches television. For this large group, the Communists fashioned the slogan "nuclear war is unthinkable."

In marketing this slogan, the Communists made great capital out of the movie *On The Beach*. As moviegoers emerged from the theater, Communist-fronters in the lobby and on the sidewalks would ask them to sign Red peace petitions.

On The Beach was a make-believe story about the end of the world. Somebody pushes the wrong button, we are propelled into nuclear war, and everybody everywhere is killed except people on Australia. As the fallout gradually approaches, the people there realize they have only two months left to live, so they spend their remaining days in drink and sin. They finally queue up for their government-issued suicide pills just before fallout reaches them, and so ends the human race.

Of course the movie is morally false, and it is scientifically false; but beyond that, it served as a vehicle of Communist propaganda because it sold the false slogan that "nuclear war is unthinkable." It played a significant role in influencing Americans to accept the three-year unilateral nuclear test ban of 1958-61. The 1963 showing of *On The Beach* on television brought about a second tidal wave of this same Red propaganda — this time to persuade us to accept the Moscow Nuclear Test Ban Treaty.

Since *On The Beach* blazed the trail, we have been treated with a whole rash of fictional hallucinations which peddle the Communist line that we are in imminent danger of *accidental* nuclear war, and therefore the U. S. should appease, retreat, and even surrender in order to avoid the risk. In 1964 movies such as *Dr. Strangelove, Seven Days in May* and *The Victors*, the bad guys are never the Communists. The villains are usually American military leaders, pictured as conspiratorial, stupid or grossly immoral.

In *Dr. Strangelove* (directed by Stanley Kubrick who also gave us *Lolita*), our military leaders are made the butt of satire, with nuclear war started by a psychotic U. S. Air Force general, and another high-ranking general portrayed as too busy having an affair with his secretary to recall the nuclear bombers. According to *The Worker*, the official Communist newspaper:

> "Nothing but disarmament can save us from the bomb. . . . It is the insane American

general . . . who orders the attack and triggers the world's destruction. . . . The Pentagon is infested . . . (with such) insanity."[6]

Such movies are selling Americans on defeatism, pacifism and the unilateral disarmament that leads to surrender to Communism.

The best-selling novel *Fail-Safe* (also made into a movie) dishes out disarmament propaganda in even heavier dosages. *Fail-Safe* is the story of how nuclear war is touched off by the accidental failure of a single computer. To convince Khrushchev that this was a genuine error and to "show our good faith", our President orders an American plane to drop a hydrogen bomb on New York City. *Fail-Safe* cannot be dismissed as fantasy. It constitutes deliberate deception of the American people. Authors, publishers and reviewers falsely boast that the story is "true" and "convincing," that a fatal accident triggering universal destruction is "inevitable," and that accidental nuclear war "ultimately will occur." Such novels and movies help to create the political climate in which Americans can be led to acquiesce in the disarmament plans the Communists have made for us. *Fail-Safe* has repeatedly been demonstrated to be completely false in its basic assumptions, by official U. S. Air Force refutations and by publications of distinguished authorities.[7] Yet the liberal press denies equal publicity to the authoritative versions.

Propaganda against nuclear tests frightened us by threats of strontium 90 in the milk, radiation in children's teeth, and the deformation of unborn babies. Dr. Edward Teller, the father of the H-bomb, exposed in his book *Our Nuclear Future* that the enormous amount of scare talk about fallout is largely Communist-inspired propaganda. He gave charts which prove that a lifetime dose of fallout from the testing of the nuclear weapons is not as dangerous as smoking one cigarette a month, having a chest X-ray once a year, or wearing a luminous dial wrist watch.[8] In *The Reader's Digest,* Dr. Teller sounded a clear alarm to the American public on this and showed that it is not fallout which is dangerous, but "fear of fallout" because this is what brought about the nuclear test moratorium which Dr. Teller said "contributed decisively to our weakness and our danger".[9]

DISARMAMENT PREVENTS WAR

Disarmament propaganda specifically designed to appeal to idealistic and church-going Americans is concentrated in the slogan "disarmament prevents war." All good people want to prevent war, and this slogan has been repeated so often that many people believe disarmament is the key. This is a fantastic achievement of the big lie, because it is contrary to all historical evidence.[10]

The waters of history are studded with the wrecks of countries which thought they could guarantee peace by disarmament. In ancient times, the Carthaginians tried to convince Rome of their sincere desire for peace by disarming, even while the Roman Senator Cato was ending each speech with the words: "Carthage must be destroyed." After Carthage had unilaterally disarmed, the

Roman legions attacked, destroyed the city, burned its libraries, killed its men, sold its women and children into slavery, and a great nation disappeared from the face of the earth.

Fortunately for Western civilization, the Greeks did not disarm in the face of the Persian peril, the Franks were not disarmed when the Arabs invaded France in the 8th Century, and European navies were not disarmed when the Turkish fleet attacked at Lepanto.

It was not an armament race, but a disarmament race, which caused World War II. Because the British Empire and the United States disarmed under the influence of the Washington and London disarmament treaties and the Kellogg Anti-War Pact, the Japanese, Nazis and Soviets knew that they were much better armed than the West, and could win great victories as soon as they triggered war. Belgium, Holland, Denmark, Norway, Latvia, Lithuania, Estonia, France and Poland thought they could avoid war by relying on peace treaties and obsolete weapons which were purely defensive. Instead, they invited attack. All were occupied and, like Carthage, some have disappeared. Fortunately, in spite of the appeasement policies of the British government, British engineers did not rely on Chamberlain's treaty with Hitler, but perfected the wonderful Spitfire airplane in time to win the Battle of Britain.

Human nature is not going to change. No sane person suggests disarming the police in order to stop gangsters and bank robbers. Since the crimes of Khrushchev far exceed the crimes of the Ca-

pone and Dillinger gangs, it would be folly to disarm as long as Communist gangsters threaten the
world.

Listen to General Thomas S. Power, distinguished head of our Strategic Air Command:

> "Any lawyer would indict disarmament as the
> arch villain of history. It has been tried again
> and again since centuries before Christ, and
> it has *always* led to war, *never* to peace. Sure
> we are in an arms race, and we had better
> win it. It's a lot better than having to win
> a shooting war."[11]

Americans should heed the wisdom of Winston
Churchill:

> "Sometimes in the past we have committed
> the folly of throwing away our arms. Under
> the mercy of Providence, and at great cost
> and sacrifice, we have been able to recreate
> them when the need arose.
> "But if we abandon our nuclear deterrent,
> there will be no second chance. To abandon
> it now would be to abandon it forever."

The key to peace was given to us by the Father
of our Country, George Washington, who said:

> "To be prepared for war is one of the most
> effectual ways of preserving peace."[12]

Chapter Six

THE NITZE AXIS

During World War II, a number of the grave-diggers, including Paul H. Nitze, worked for the Board of Economic Warfare. This agency learned that the German troops used rabbit skins to keep warm on the Russian Front. So, the Board of Economic Warfare developed its preemptive project to win the war in a hurry. It was to buy up all the rabbits in Europe, and thereby cause the German troops to freeze to death in Russia. Of course, the well-known ability of rabbits to multiply, especially when their owners are encouraged by dollars, soon caused the rabbit population of Europe to exceed even the funds of the bureaucrats.

This hare-brained scheme for winning the war by cornering the market in rabbits was sound and logical compared with the disarmament schemes of the gravediggers in our Government today.

In April 1960 at Asilomar, California a meeting was held which affects the life and freedom of every American. Officially dubbed the Asilomar National Strategy Seminar, this was one of the most important groups ever assembled on national strategy. The U. S. Army spent thousands of dollars to bring together more than 500 scholars and strategy experts.

On April 29, Paul H. Nitze, a New York investment banker, read a paper to the Asilomar National Strategy Seminar. He said that, in a poker game with several players, the most dangerous hand is "not the worst hand but the second best hand. With the second best hand, one is tempted to follow up the betting, but if one does, one gets clobbered."

Nitze applied the poker analogy to U. S. nuclear strategy and launched the notion — for which there is no basis in all military history — that it is safer to be weak than strong. He then made this sensational Proposal: (1) that we give up trying to achieve "a true Class A nuclear capability;" (2) that "we scrap the fixed base vulnerable systems that have their principal utility as components of a Class A capability;" (3) that we turn our retaliatory systems over to NATO; and (4) that the UN should have the "ultimate power of decision on the use of these systems."[1]

Nitze further proposed that the U. S. disarm "in a series of unilateral actions designed to produce reciprocal action . . . on the part of our enemies." His plan for strategic disarmament of the United States was justified on the basis that "the Soviet Union would be *invited* to take reciprocal action," and "it would be *hoped*" that the Soviet would do so. Thus, under the Nitze Asilomar Proposal, the U. S. would deliberately leave itself *no choice but surrender, no effective deterrent to destruction.* Everything would be staked on the "hope" that the Soviets would disarm *after we do.*

The new Kennedy-Johnson Administration,

elected seven months later, couldn't wait to get
Nitze into the official family. In spite of his shocking disarmament proposals — or maybe because of
them — Nitze was selected to be Assistant Secretary of Defense even before Kennedy and Johnson
were sworn in.

In October 1963 Nitze was promoted to Secretary of the Navy. His explanations of his Asilomar
Proposal were so ambiguous that the Senate
Armed Services Committee passing on his nomi-
nation took the unusual step of requiring him to
submit his testimony under oath. Nitze tried to
excuse his Asilomar paper on the ground he was
not speaking seriously. It is too much of a strain
on our credulity to believe that a man such as Paul
Nitze would pull a practical joke on matters of
life and death before the most distinguished and
highranking audience of strategists and policy-
makers ever assembled.

Furthermore, Nitze had also been the chairman
of a report issued by the National Council of
Churches which paralleled the third and fourth
phases of his Asilomar Proposal. Nitze tried to
explain this away by saying he had disagreed with
the report — although it was issued under his name
and he had not published any dissent.

For the Kennedy-Johnson Administration to ap-
point the author of such shocking disarmament
notions to top Defense Department jobs is like
turning over the security of our homes and our
country to the far-out plans division of the Disarmament Agency.

The gravediggers who swarmed into Washing-

ton with the Kennedy-Johnson Administration lit
on Nitze's Asilomar Proposal like hungry flies on
syrup. Nitze's unique contribution was that he
took the wildest notions of the most radical world-
government pacifist disarmers, and he provided a
practical plan to make these schemes work — and
then he covered it with all the semantic camou-
flage needed to fool Congress and the public. This
paper written by one little-known gravedigger became the Disarmament Manifesto of President
Kennedy's New Frontier and of President Johnson's Great Society.

As soon as the Kennedy-Johnson Administration
was inaugurated, the gravediggers began to implement the Nitze Proposal. Under phases (1)
and (2) of Nitze's Proposal, we are scrapping 90
percent of our nuclear striking power, but this is
disguised as discarding "vulnerable systems" for
"secure systems." In phases (3) and (4), Nitze
proposes to surrender all control over our remaining nuclear weapons, but this is disguised as
"building a variety of secure, purely retaliatory
systems" as to which "we multilateralize the command."[2]

The specific implementation of the Nitze Proposal is spelled out in the McNamara Gap. For
four years, with increasing momentum, McNamara's policies have carried out Nitze's plans.
Documentary evidence that Nitze's unilateral disarmament is indeed the present policy of the
Kennedy-Johnson Administration was provided by
two recent articles written by members of the
Nitze Axis for *Foreign Affairs,* the official publica-

tion of the powerful Council on Foreign Relations. The first,[3] by McGeorge Bundy, Special Assistant to the President for National Security Affairs, expresses concern that our "nuclear strength can be provocative." Bundy praises the Presidential decision against a nuclear weapon system "which required a base abroad and evoked a real or pretended charge of encirclement from Moscow." He applauds the President for not referring to the Communist world as "the enemy." As proof of gravedigger Bundy's consistent wrongness on the subject of Communism, consider what he told the nation by television on October 14, 1962, — after Soviet offensive missiles had been installed in Cuba:

> "I know there is no present evidence, and I think there is no present likelihood that the Cubans and the Cuban Government and the Soviet Government would in combination attempt to install major offensive capability."

In the April 1964 issue of *Foreign Affairs*, there is an article called "Our Defense Needs" by Roswell L. Gilpatric, Deputy Secretary of Defense in the Kennedy-Johnson Administration for three years, and long-time number-two man to McNamara in the Pentagon. In his article, he proposes the most drastic plan for the unilateral disarmament of the United States ever published by a person with such continuous and close relationships with the very highest levels in the Administration.

Here is Gilpatric's proposal: (1) "all manned bombers retired from active deployment;" (2)

"only warning systems . . . in Alaska, Greenland and Scotland . . . manned interceptors . . . and all other bomber defense and warning systems would be phased out . . ."; (3) "no production or deployment of anti-ballistic-missile systems in the absence of Soviet moves to proceed beyond experimental installations of such systems;" (4) "an annual level of defense expenditure about 25 percent below the current rate."[4]

Gilpatric resigned as Deputy Secretary of Defense after it became known that he voted to award the largest Government contract in history to a Texas manufacturer who was not the low bidder and did not offer the best product. However, he still speaks with authority for the gravediggers, and *Foreign Affairs* is as much the official publication of the gravediggers as *Pravda* is of the Communists. On September 10, 1964, Lyndon Johnson appointed Gilpatric a consultant on "major international problems."

The bait on the Gilpatric hook for the politicians is the proposed cut in annual defense spending of 25 percent or about $12.5 billion. This bait was restated by McNamara at the 1964 Democratic National Convention where it was eagerly grabbed by politicians anxious to spend this money on domestic projects which buy votes.

The Nitze and Gilpatric proposals are substantially identical. They outline the actual present defense policy under McNamara. The Nitze and Gilpatric proposals both advocate bringing U. S. strategic power down to a low level by U. S. unilateral actions. Both proposals seek to circumvent the safeguards of the U. S. Constitution. The Nitze paper considers the U. S. Senate as the prime stumbling block which can be avoided if the Administration will merely take unilateral actions. Gilpatric emphasizes the superior wisdom of the bureaucrats, especially of the gravediggers, and admits that he resents having a veto imposed on them by the American people.[5]

Chapter Seven

PUGWASH BRAINWASH

It is seldom that murderers and gravediggers meet together to make their plans. Such a unique meeting took place in Moscow November 27 to December 5, 1960 when Khrushchev and 21 Soviet Communists met with U. S. scientists attending the Sixth Pugwash Conference.

The Pugwash Conferences are high-level meetings which bring together select top-level nuclear scientists and governmental advisers from both sides of the Iron Curtain. The Pugwash Conferences take their name from the location of the first Conference held in 1957 at the home of Cyrus S. Eaton, multi-millionaire American industrialist and investment banker, in Pugwash, Nova Scotia. Thus, the Pugwashers parallel the Bilderbergers, the secret group of kingmakers who named their organization after the site of their first conclave at the Bilderberg Hotel in the Netherlands in 1954.

Also like the Bilderbergers, Pugwashers shrink from publicity. Cyrus Eaton has insisted that 12 out of 13 Pugwash Conferences be held outside the United States in secrecy from the American press — but not of course from the Soviet agents who participate. As the chief financial backer of the Pugwash Conferences, Cyrus Eaton was described by the Senate Internal Security Subcommittee in these words:

"Eaton's fawning attitude toward the Soviet
Union is best exemplified by his unbridled
adoration for Premier Nikita S. Khrushchev,
in strange contrast to his wholesale condem-
nation of the American Government and its
leaders."[1]

Other prime movers in the Pugwash Conferences
include Lord Bertrand (rather Red than dead)
Russell, the late French Communist P. Joliet-
Curie, and the Canadian defector to Poland Leo-
pold Infeld.

The most important of all the Pugwash Conferences took place in Moscow in November-Decem-
ber, 1960.

The Moscow Pugwash Conference was attended
by 24 prominent U. S. scientists, many of whom
soon were given "secret" and even "top secret"
U. S. security clearances. The American group
was headed by Dr. Jerome B. Wiesner and Dr.
Walt W. Rostow, who within weeks after the Pugwash Conference became leading policy planners
of the Kennedy-Johnson Administration.

At the Moscow Pugwash Conference, Walt W.
Rostow gave the closing address under the title
"The Long Run and the Short Run,"[2] which reveals the thinking of the Pugwashers in general
and of the foreign policy advisers of the Kennedy-
Johnson Administration in particular. Here are
the key ideas:

1) "Accidental war is a present danger." This
frightening theme of *accidental* war was intro-
duced at the first Pugwash Conference by Soviet
"academician" Topchiev. Since then it has become

a basic assumption of the "rather Red than dead" group and of the novels and movies designed to make us believe that "nuclear war is unthinkable."

2) "A completion of the test-ban negotiation . . . should . . . open the way to the step beyond." Rostow here forecast that the Kennedy-Johnson Administration would push hard for the Test Ban. It is clear that Rostow, as chief foreign policy planner of the Administration, looked upon the Treaty as starting us on the escalator to the "step beyond." Americans would like to know what is the *step beyond.*

The other chief U. S. representative at the Moscow Pugwash Conference, Dr. Jerome B. Wiesner, outlined a comprehensive program for disarmament and transferring our military strength to an international agency. He urged the Soviet Union to develop a defense system which could absorb a surprise attack, and he suggested that the Soviets harden their own missile sites.[3]

The Pugwash papers constitute a mass of highly-specialized and technical propaganda designed to appeal to the gravediggers and the scientists. It is all enveloped in so much egghead lingo that Americans have a hard time coming to grips with the issues, but it can be fairly summarized as "rather Red than dead." Pugwashers have spread this thinking through the highest echelons of our government, business, scientific and academic communities. President Johnson told the 12th Pugwash Conference in India that its program "will be studied thoroughly by me and by this Government in our continued effort to achieve workable disarmament."[4]

When these gravediggers find it embarrassing to let it be known that their plans will lead to surrender, they fall back on the slogan: "Nuclear parity will promote peace." According to this curious false assumption, all the Soviets want is to feel secure against possible aggression; and, therefore, we should correct any nuclear imbalance in favor of America, and work toward nuclear equality between America and the Soviet Union. On this absurd theory, we should erect a national monument to Klaus Fuchs for supplying our atomic secrets to the Soviets!

Yet Robert Strange McNamara believes this nonsense. He said:

> "This is why a nuclear exchange confined to military targets seems more possible, not less, when *both* sides have a sure second strike capability. Then you might have a more stable balance of terror."[5] (Emphasis added).

The fatal fallacy in this "nuclear parity" assumption is that nuclear parity is precisely the condition which will promote a surprise attack. It is not true that neither side could win a nuclear war. The Soviets could achieve the calculated win through the advantage of surprise attack — and this is the grave the Pugwashers are digging for Americans.

Chapter Eight

FAR TO THE LEFT OF EVEN HUMPHREY

After the inauguration of the Kennedy-Johnson Administration, the gravediggers swarmed into Washington, eager to move full speed ahead in implementing their plans. Except for Alger Hiss, most of the appeasement crowd from the old Truman-Acheson Administration was back on the payroll within a few months. By September 1961, the gravediggers felt confident enough of their power to show their hand and reveal what they plan for America's future.

"A RADICAL PROGRAM"

The State Department led off in September 1961 with the issuance of Publication 7277 called *Freedom From War: The United States Program for General and Complete Disarmament in a Peaceful World.*

According to this policy statement of the State Department, officially published by the Government Printing Office, the United States Government intends to abolish our Army, our Navy, our Air Force, and our nuclear weapons in three stages, at the end of which time we will be subject to a "United Nations Peace Force." Thus, the official policy of the Kennedy-Johnson Administration, as stated in this sensational 20-page official document, calls for:

> "The disbanding of all national armed forces and the prohibition of their reestablishment in any form whatsoever other than those required to preserve internal order and for contributions to a United Nations Peace force;
>
> "The elimination from national arsenals of all armaments, including all weapons of mass destruction and the means for their delivery, other than those required for a United Nations Peace Force and for maintaining internal order . . . "[1]

On April 18, 1962, our Government announced its proposals to implement this State Department disarmament policy. Under this Geneva proposal, our country will be disarmed 30 percent in three years, and totally disarmed in nine years, at which time we will be completely subject to a permanent "UN Peace Force." This policy has been pushed vigorously ever since, not only by the State Department, but the U. S. Arms Control and Disarmament Agency. Khrushchev responded by moving his missiles to Cuba.

Those who are forwarned are forearmed. Americans are fortunate to know in advance what happens to a country under control of the UN Peace Force. In the Congo in 1961 and 1962, the UN Peace Force, including savage Gurkha mercenaries, attacked hospitals, schools and civilians in order to force the anti-Communist, Christian government of Tshombe to surrender to the Gizenga-Adoula-Gbenye Communist coalition faction.

There is no logical or factual basis for assuming that any future UN Peace Force — to which the State Department is planning to subject American citizens — would behave any differently.

It is particularly significant that the anonymous gravediggers who authored State Department Publication 7277 did not bother to disguise the lineage of this nefarious scheme. Any American who can read can easily prove to his own satisfaction that the granddaddy of this disarmament plan is the Communists' own proposal for "General and Complete Disarmament" which was presented personally by Khrushchev to the United Nations exactly two years earlier. The striking similarities between the Soviet and the State Department plans are obvious in objectives, in specifics and in wording. Khrushchev boasted in his speech to the UN in 1959 that "This is a radical program."

It certainly was! Our nation's press almost unanimously greeted Khrushchev's proposal with the skepticism it deserved.

Yet, two years later, this same plan turned up as the official policy of our State Department! The Nitze Proposal and the Moscow Pugwash Conference were the instruments through which the gravediggers turned Khrushchev's own pet project into the policy of the U. S. State Department. This was the crowning achievement of the Soviet weapon of "opinion subversion."

On June 10, 1963, President Kennedy made a Commencement speech at American University in which he confirmed that our national policy is disarmament. His exact words were these:

"Our primary long-range interest in Geneva
. . . is general and complete disarmament —
designed to take place by stages."

"THE LIBERAL PAPERS"

By 1962 the gravediggers in the Kennedy-Johnson Administration crawled even farther out of the woodwork and make a frank attempt to sell the most radical disarmament ideas to Congress, educators and students. For at least two years, about 40 gravedigger intellectuals, most of whom became influential advisers in the Kennedy-Johnson Administration, had been working on "The Liberal Project" with a group of 35 Democratic Congressmen identified in the book as "far to the left of well-known Democratic Senators such as (Hubert) Humphrey."

In March 1962 their work was published under the title *The Liberal Papers*. In order to merchandise their disarmament propaganda, the gravediggers hid behind a magic name. They persuaded Congressman James Roosevelt, eldest son of President Franklin Roosevelt, to lend his name as "editor." The gravediggers knew that most Americans did not know of Jimmy Roosevelt's own far left record.

On March 11, 1946 he attacked Winston Churchill's "Iron Curtain" speech given at the invitation of President Truman at Fulton, Missouri. On March 16, 1946 he criticized President Truman for requesting Stalin to pull Red troops out of Iran. On April 2, 1946 he said Russia should have the Dardanelles. On June 4, 1947 Roosevelt denounced the "Truman Doctrine of aid to Greece and Turkey". Since 1959 Jimmy Roosevelt has led a one-man campaign to abolish the U. S. House Committee on Un-American Activities.

The Liberal Papers is an amazing revelation of what goes on in the eggheads of the gravediggers who are disarming America. Some of the following proposals of this admitted "far to the left" Democratic-sponsored book have already been carried out and others are expected after the presidential election in 1964: (1) We "should begin right now to close down" our missile bases throughout Europe; (2) "An agreement by the nuclear powers to ban test explosions"; (3) We should demilitarize West Germany, recognize East Germany, and dismantle NATO; (4) We would make the DEW line — our great northern radar warning system — bi-directional and invite the Soviets to "plug in" so they could have all the advantages of our installations; (5) We should recognize Red China and sponsor her admission to the United Nations; (6) We should turn over Formosa, Quemoy and Matsu to Red China by the ruse of pretending to give them to the UN for five years; and (7) The U. S. Government should give financial aid to Red China and other Communist countries.

The Liberal Papers specifically espouses the "rather Red than dead" views of Lord Bertrand Russell. The book calls for "unilateral" acts of disarmament by the U. S. in the hope that they will be reciprocated by the Soviets. *The Liberal Papers* should be renamed "Roosevelt's Munich."

Chamberlain never did as much for Hitler as is here proposed under the name of liberalism to be done for Khrushchev and Mao. Senator Barry Goldwater said its theme is: "Keep giving in. Keep yielding."

Who are some of the authors of the disarmament schemes in *The Liberal Papers?* Marcus Raskin, identified in Chapter One as having "taken a leading role in the development of the Project", is credited as the author of the State Department program for General and Complete Disarmament of the United States by 1970.[2] During the two-year preparation of *The Liberal Papers*, U. S. gravedigger Raskin turned up on the payroll of eight "far to the left" Congressmen in 1960 and on the payroll of six "far to the left" Congressmen in 1961.

Another pair of U. S. gravediggers who wrote chapters for *The Liberal Papers* are Arthur Waskow and Walter Millis. As a sample of their thinking read the following excerpt from the report they wrote to guide William C. Foster and Averell Harriman when the latter negotiated the Test Ban Treaty in Moscow:

> "Whether we admit it to ourselves or not, we benefit enormously from the capacity of the Soviet Police State to keep law and order over the 500 million-odd Russians and the many additional millions in the satellite States. The breakup of the Russian Communist empire today would doubtless be conducive to freedom, but it would be a good deal more catastrophic for world order, than

was the breakup of the Austro-Hungarian Empire in 1918."[3]

The Liberal Papers should have galvanized the American people into action against the gravediggers who are working to help Khrushchev bury us. This radical book fully corroborates a recent penetrating study which demonstrates conclusively that "liberalism is the ideology of Western suicide."[4] Liberal ideology demands that the West abandon all weapons which could effectively defend us against the Communist conquest of the world. The gravediggers work fanatically for unilateral nuclear disarmament, and it is only occasionally, as in *The Liberal Papers*, that they deign to let the American people know what they plan for our future.

Chapter Nine

CRAWLING TO MOSCOW

In 1959 in the great novel *Advise and Consent,* the most disliked and distrusted Senator repeatedly exclaimed:

> "I had rather crawl to Moscow than perish under a bomb."

The liberal claque that wants to crawl is always sounding off about the terrible danger of the "escalation" of nuclear weapons.

What the American people should be most concerned about is the escalation of appeasement. Appeasement has escalated so rapidly in the last four years that the Kennedy-Johnson Administration sent Averell Harriman to crawl on his knees to Moscow to obtain the Nuclear Test Ban Treaty. What was considered unpatriotic in 1959, was in 1963 represented as necessary lest the Red leaders take offense.

This escalation of appeasement is shown numerically by the progressive concessions made to persuade the Soviets to sign the test ban treaty. Five years before, we demanded 180 internationally-manned detection stations and 20 annual on-site inspections. Later we reduced our demands to 19 stations, then to 3 unmanned "black boxes." We reduced the on-site inspections to 12, then 8, then 7, then 5. When Averell Harriman signed the

Nuclear Test Ban Treaty in Moscow in 1963, it brought us full circle to an acceptance of the original Soviet position of no inspection and no detection stations whatsoever.

The Moscow Nuclear Test Ban Treaty represents a monumental achievement of Soviet propaganda. President Kennedy said on November 8, 1961:

> "The Soviet Union prepared to test [nuclear weapons] while we were at the table negotiating with them. If they fooled us once it is their fault; if they fool us twice, it is our fault."

The Moscow Test Ban Treaty means fooling us twice. It repeats the same tragic mistake of the nuclear test moratorium of 1958-61, which cost us our nuclear supremacy.

On March 2, 1962, President Kennedy added:

> "We know enough about broken negotiations, secret preparations and the [Soviet] advantages gained from a long test series never to offer again an uninspected moratorium."

But the Moscow Nuclear Test Ban Treaty of 1963 has no provisions at all for inspection.

By signing the Moscow Test Ban Treaty of 1963, the Kennedy-Johnson Administration accepted a permanent military status that is second best to the USSR. This is made clear by the statement of the Joint Chiefs of Staff to the Senate Committees on August 15, 1963:

> "It is indicated that the USSR is ahead of the United States in the high-yield (tens of megatons) technology, in weapons effect knowledge derived from high-yield nuclear

devices and in the yield/weight ratios of high-yield devices; and that the USSR lags somewhat behind the United States at low yields. "If . . . both sides faithfully observe its [the Moscow Test Ban Treaty's] provisions . . . the United States would not be able to overtake the present advantage which the USSR probably has in the high-yield weapons field, whereas the Soviets, by underground testing, could probably retrieve in time any lead which we may presently have in the low-yield tactical field."

The Joint Chiefs thus served notice that the U. S. has surrendered its position of world supremacy in the technology of the most powerful weaponry, and is guaranteeing to the Soviets strategic supremacy sufficient to destroy the United States.[1] Unless the Johnson-McNamara decisions are reversed, fatal events will not wait for our grandchildren or children. We ourselves will witness the decline and fall of the United States. For — as the Joint Chiefs have warned us in one additional unanimous judgment:

"Militant Communism remains dedicated to the destruction of our society."[2]

The Johnson-McNamara gravediggers are putting all our defense eggs in the Minuteman-Polaris basket. They have NEVER, repeat, NEVER, tested the warhead or exploding part of any Minuteman or other Air Force missile upon which McNamara relies. The Polaris missile has been test-fired only *once* with its atomic warhead. General Curtis LeMay, Air Force Chief of Staff, General Thomas Power, head of the Strategic Air

Command, Admiral George W. Anderson, when chief of Naval Operations, and Major General Barry Goldwater have all criticized the refusal to permit testing of our missiles.[3]

The great Soviet tests of 1961-62 revealed the electromagnetic pulse effect. This is a very powerful surge of electricity which accompanies every large nuclear blast. It fuses wires and burns out circuits many miles from where the bomb explodes. Nobody knows if our untested retaliatory weapons could function if a Soviet super hydrogen bomb landed within 1,000 miles of them.

McNamara's failure to test properly the Edsel car was damaging only to Ford, but a continuation of his failure to test our missile warheads and defenses under the Moscow Test Ban Treaty will be fatal to the American Republic.

During the years prior to World War II, for reasons of "safety" and "economy", our country failed to test its submarine torpedoes with live warheads. As a result, when we suddenly found ourselves in a vast naval war with Japan, our brave submarine crews were sent into combat with torpedoes which did not explode on contact with enemy ships. In the Moscow Test Ban Treaty, we repeat this dangerous failure to test. In the last five years, the Soviets have tested in the atmosphere 72 more nuclear devices than we have tested.[4] Their nuclear weapons and defenses are tested — ours are not.

To prevent World War III, we have two alternatives: (1) to rely on American military strength, or (2) to rely on Communist promises. By the Moscow Treaty, the Administration chose to rely on Communist promises in spite of the evidence that all Communists practice what Lenin taught:

"Promises are like piecrusts, made to be broken."[5]

The Soviet Union has broken its word to every country to which it ever gave a signed promise, except that Stalin fulfilled and overfulfilled his treaty with Hitler because of fear of Hitler's superior military power. The Panmunjom Agreement was promptly and repeatedly violated by the Reds. Just as a confirmed alcoholic is not cured by taking one more drink, so a confirmed treaty-breaker is not cured by signing one more treaty.

The great illusion at the conferences of Teheran, Yalta and Potsdam was that, if we would just give the Soviet Union pro-Communist countries along her borders, the Soviets would "feel secure" and would give up their aggressive intentions. Everyone now admits this was as futile as trying to appease Hitler with Austria and Czechoslovakia. The Moscow Test Ban Treaty makes the same mistake. It rests on the vain hope that, if we permit the Soviets to surpass us in large nuclear weapons, if we halt our own development so they will stay ahead of us, then the Soviets will "feel secure" and abandon their effort to bury us.

Khrushchev did not bother to conceal his belief that the Moscow Nuclear Test Ban Treaty is a victory for world Communism. He boasted that it was a "victory" for world Communism that it "would perpetuate . . . the . . . liquidation [of American nuclear monopoly]."

Chapter Ten

"THE PUBLIC IS TOO DUMB TO UNDERSTAND"

Franklin Roosevelt's chief assistant, Harry Hopkins, revealed his contempt for the American people in these profane words: "The public is too damned dumb to understand." This was the formula Hopkins applied so ruthlessly during World War II when he gave Stalin $11 billion of American lend-lease equipment without requesting even the concessions Stalin was willing to make. Unknown to American voters, much of what Hopkins sent was for postwar use. Handouts to the Soviet Union included secret blueprints, heavy water, uranium, etc., for making the atomic bomb, plus the secret American plates and processes for printing German occupation money.[1]

The Hopkins formula that "The public is too damned dumb to understand" was used again by the Roosevelt Administration to suppress the Van Vliet Report which told of one of the most heinous crimes in modern history, the Katyn Forest Massacre. This report by Colonels Van Vliet and Stewart described the Soviet murder of some 10,000 Polish leaders who had been shot in the back of the head and buried in mass graves. The two Army officers were ordered under pain of court martial never to reveal the truth to anyone — in order that the Roosevelt Administration could propagate the false myth that the Soviet Union was a "peace-loving democracy."[2]

The Roosevelt and Truman Administrations used the Hopkins formula to suppress the official papers of Teheran, Yalta, and Potsdam. 20 years later, the American people are still considered "too dumb" to be trusted with the record of those three important World War II Conferences. The Truman Administration applied the Hopkins formula to the 1947 Wedemeyer Report which could have saved China and Korea from Communism had its recommendations been followed.[3]

Under the Kennedy-Johnson Administration, the Harry Hopkins formula has been revived and intensified. The people are considered not only stupid, but dangerous. American military, foreign, economic and domestic policies are now made by reports which the American people either are not permitted to read, or which we find out about only by accident. High officials of the Kennedy-Johnson Administration believe that "prevailing public opinion" will most probably be "destructively wrong at the critical junctures," and that if the people find out about plans for accommodation, they may "impose a veto upon the judgments of informed and responsible public officials."[4]

Here are the secret documents written by the gravediggers of a strong America which together make up the hidden program of the Kennedy-Johnson Administration.

THE SECRET FULBRIGHT
MEMORANDUM

Reported to have been written at the behest
of Adam Yarmolinsky for Senator J. William Fulbright, this document laid down the policy called
"muzzling the military." It was responsible for the
silencing by the Kennedy Administration of all
anti-Communist speeches and statements of generals and admirals who tried to warn us of the
Communist threat to our country. The Memorandum sought to prevent the participation by anyone in the government or the military in anti-
Communist schools, seminars or lectures.

This "muzzling of the military" was carried to
such lengths that one of the services had to resort
to keeping its intelligence officers informed by
means of a bootlegged reading or "Accession List,"
mailed on plain paper in unmarked envelopes.
This was necessary to prevent the civilian gravediggers in the Pentagon from sacking the patriotic
officers who circulated information on the evils of
Communism.

Not only did the Fulbright Memorandum pro-
hibit military officers from educating their men
about Communism, but it placed our military
establishment under the strictures of an official
refusal to be realistic about the facts of Communist
advance. In accord with this Memorandum,[5] General Decker, Army Chief of Staff, was forbidden
to explain to the Army chaplains on January 30,
1961, the falsity of the made-in-Moscow slogan,

"rather Red than dead." In a February 1, 1961 speech, General Trudeau was forbidden to quote Khrushchev's statement "we will bury you." Generals and admirals were forbidden to describe Communism as "vicious," or "treacherous," or a "threat," or to warn of the menace of "Soviet infiltration" or about "the Communist conspiracy directed toward absolute, universal domination of the world;" to speak of "victory" or to say we must "emerge victorious." Our military leaders are forbidden to refer to the anti-religious nature of Communism or to speak of Communism as "godless."

The Fulbright Memorandum was much more than the "muzzling of the military." It laid the groundwork for the "no win" policy which has deteriorated into the "sure-lose" policy of the Kennedy-Johnson Administration.[6] This remarkable document said that Cuba and Laos were dangers — not because they represented Soviet victories and the enslavement of more millions of people — but because they aroused Americans to the Communist danger.

Although the Fulbright Memorandum was put into effect by the Pentagon as official policy, both the Pentagon and Senator Fulbright tried to prevent the American people from knowing of its existence! The only reason we know the text of the Fulbright Memorandum is that Senator Strom Thurmond somehow got a copy and read it into the *Congressional Record* on August 2, 1961, after which Fulbright was forced to confirm it.

THE SECRET ROSTOW-MOSCOW REPORT

The Rostow Report is a master plan on foreign policy and disarmament written by Walt W. Rostow, chairman of the State Department Policy Planning Board. It embodies some notions its author has entertained ever since he made a pilgrimage to Moscow in December, 1960 — just after the Kennedy-Johnson election victory in November and before Rostow assumed his post in the State Department. Rostow comes from a Socialist family. He was named for Walt Whitman, the favorite poet of U. S. Socialists; his brother, Eugene Debs Rostow, was named after the longtime Socialist Party candidate for President.

The Rostow Report is the bureaucratic implementation of the "no win" policy so well described by Walt W. Rostow in a speech at Fort Bragg, North Carolina, just prior to his appointment as policy-planning chairman in the U. S. State Department:

> "The victory we seek . . . will not be a victory
> of the United States over the Soviet Union.
> It will not be a victory of capitalism over
> socialism."[7]

According to the Rostow Report, U. S. foreign policy should be based on the assumption that differences between us and the Soviet Union will gradually "wither away," because the Communists are "mellowing" and going through a process of "evolution" in which the Soviet Union will abandon its goal of world conquest and grow close to the United States in ideals and aspirations.

The Rostow Report says that we must abandon our first-strike weapons in order not to arouse the suspicions of the Soviets or make them jittery. The Report says we must not seek victory of the United States over the Soviet Union or of capitalism over Communism, that we must treat Communist governments gently and not attack or criticize the satellites, that we must never give any encouragement to revolts behind the Iron Curtain, that we should deny U. S. foreign aid to countries in order to force them into coalition governments with the Communists as was done in Loas, and that we must work toward general and complete disarmament. The Rostow Report obviously recognized that the American people would be shocked at these proposals because it calls upon the Administration to embark on a systematic publicity campaign in order to sell them to Congress and to the American people.

There is plenty of evidence that this Rostow-Moscow Report has been put into effect and these are now the policies of our government. The Rostow Report makes it clear why our government does not raise a finger to help the Cuban exiles, but instead arrests the Cuban patriots who want to free Cuba. This is why the United States sent guns and planes to shoot down Tshombe's supporters in Katanga, why we forced the anti-Communists in Laos to go into a coalition government with the Communists, why the State Department issued a report on Hungary that reads like a product of Kadar's own propaganda machine, and why we lavish billions on the cruel dictators

Tito, Gomulka and Sukarno.

Yet the Rostow Report itself has been success-fully kept secret and the American people are not permitted to see this document which determines our foreign policy. The only reason we know of its existence is that in June, 1962, one of the out-standing newspaper reporters in the country, Wil-lard Edwards of the *Chicago Tribune,* published two articles summarizing the Report and quoting from it, which Senator Everett Dirksen read into the *Congressional Record.*[8]

Disclosure of the Rostow Report caused a storm in Congress and Rostow was called before the Senate Foreign Relations Committee to answer questions. Rostow did not deny the basic facts about his Report. Like members of Cosa Nostra, he refused to answer. He invoked instead the dubious constitutional claim of "executive privi-lege," commonly referred to as the "executive fifth amendment." One of the questions Rostow de-clined to answer was whether or not the document used the word "mellowing" with reference to So-viet Russia.

Despite strenuous efforts on the part of Senators of both parties, the Johnson Administration still thinks that "the public is too dumb" to be per-mitted to read the Rostow Report.

THE SECRET CIA REPORT
ON VIET NAM

Any illusion which might have been held that the Rostow Report had "withered away" was rude-ly dispelled on August 23, 1964 with the announcement of a hitherto-secret CIA Report on Viet Nam. Reports of the Central Intelligence Agency are never made public, and this one was revealed only because the CIA knew the *Chicago Tribune* had obtained a copy, and the State Department wanted to blunt the impact of the news by putting out a coverup story.

When you cut through the usual bureaucratic doubletalk, the CIA Report turned out to be a current application of the Rostow-Moscow plan. The CIA Report states that the Soviet Union, because of economic stress and difficulties with Red China, is losing its hostility to the West and is seeking an "amiable" relationship with the United States. This comforting theme brushes off the bellicose threats of Khrushchev as a kind of international campaign oratory.[9]

The CIA Report expresses the belief that the USSR in the future will diminish "the vigor of its revolutionary effect outside the Communist world." No evidence is presented for this amazing statement, which cannot be reconciled with the facts of the establishment of a Soviet missile base in Cuba, recent Communist subversion and terrorism in Africa, Southeast Asia, Latin America and in the Harlem riots.

When the CIA Report treats of Viet Nam we see further implementation of the Rostow-Moscow line that we must not seek victory, and that we should encourage more coalition governments such as we forced upon the Congo and Laos. The CIA Report states about Viet Nam: "There remains serious doubt that victory can be won," a "prolonged stalemate" is the most we can anticipate, and the only solution for the situation in Vietnam is "some kind of negotiated settlement".

After publication of this Report, the CIA tried to minimize its importance in order to forestall a public outcry. The fact remains, however, that this 47-page report was marked "Secret" and circulated in the White House, National Security Council, and the State and Defense Departments.

THE HIDDEN BALL PLAY

Our present soft policy in the economic cold war is outlined by another secret document: the Ball Report, written by Under Secretary of State George W. Ball and co-authored by top Administration officials in the White House.[10] The thesis of this Report is that we must "seek an accommodation with the Soviet Union." It advocates a vast increase of U. S. trade with Communist countries and that we undertake to persuade other free-enterprise countries to engage in East-West trade, even in strategic items. The Ball Report urges Congress to repeal the Battle Act and other laws prohibiting strategic war goods and credits to the Communist bloc. The Ball Report recommends granting authority to the President to suspend tariffs designed to prevent the import of cheap slave-made goods from the Communist bloc.

The Ball Report is the master plan for the foreign economic policy of the Johnson Administration. Yet Under Secretary Ball has refused to permit the American people to read his Report and has refused even to make it available to the House Select Committee on Export Control.

THE SECRET REUTHER MEMORANDUM

Walter and Victor Reuther called on Attorney General Robert Kennedy in the fall of 1961 and presented an oral blueprint to destroy conservative activities in America. This conversation was followed up on December 19, 1961, when a 24-page memorandum was given to Kennedy. The writer was identified as Victor Reuther, the same man who had visited and worked in the Soviet Union in 1933 from where he had written a letter to a pal in the United States ending with the words: "Carry on the fight for a Soviet America."

The secret Reuther Memorandum was distributed to high Administration officials and to "certain sympathetic Senators and Congressmen." It called upon the Kennedy-Johnson Administration to initiate several courses of action:

1) Crush "the radical right inside the Armed Services." By Reuther's definition, the "radical right" includes anyone who believes Communism is a danger. In the armed forces, it specifically includes anyone such as General James Van Fleet who has a distinguished record of fighting the Communists from Greece and Turkey to Korea.

2) Change the Attorney General's subversive list to add conservative and anti-Communist organizations to the Communist fronts already listed.

3) Use the power of the Internal Revenue Service to remove tax-exemption from conservative religious and educational organizations.

4) Use the power of the Federal Communications Commission to keep conservative programs off radio and television stations.

5) Curb the activities of J. Edgar Hoover who "exaggerates the domestic Communist menace at every turn."

The Reuther Memorandum was promptly put into effect by the Kennedy-Johnson Administration. It was not until almost two years later that the American people learned of the existence and text of this anti-anti-Communist document.[11]

THE SECRET PHOENIX PAPER

For many months, rumors had floated around Washington that a secret document was being circulated in high official circles advocating a new policy of disarmament and collaboration with Communists. But it was not until a scoop appeared in *U. S. News and World Report* of November 18, 1963, that the American people first learned of the existence of the secret Phoenix Paper written by Vincent R. Rock for the U. S. Arms Control and Disarmament Agency. Only a few copies had been published at a cost of $78,600. It is extremely difficult for American citizens to secure this report, both because of the scarcity of copies and because the flyleaf warned: "Not to be quoted at length, abstracted, or reproduced without the specific permission of the Institute for Defense Analyses."

The Phoenix Paper calls upon the United States to reject a policy of military superiority over the Soviet Union, which under previous administrations had been the basic policy of the U. S. and NATO. This policy successfully kept us out of a hot war. General Thomas S. Power, Commander-in-Chief of the U. S. Strategic Air Command, testified before the Senate Armed Services Committee on September 6, 1963:

> "Our formula to prevent this [nuclear war] has been a successful one to date, and it is a really simple formula. We have had overwhelming military superiority to the point where it is ridiculous for Mr. Khrushchev to even seriously contemplate attacking this country. Now I maintain that it is possible to hold this type of lead, and that is what I recommend."

The Phoenix Paper plainly calls upon the United States to abandon this successful formula and trade it in for "parity" of military force with the Soviet Union. It tells us to discard our old objectives of "containment" and "co-existence" in favor of a "detente" or "interdependence" between the U. S. and the USSR.[12] The Phoenix Paper even calls upon us to consider "unification" with the Soviet Union.

The Phoenix Paper is unique not only for the fantastic policies it suggests, but for the double-dealing way it recommends that they be carried out. Thus, the Phoenix Study advises the President not to announce that he intends to disarm America because this might not be popular with Congress or the people. Instead, the President is advised to push for a tax cut — which is always popular — so that our military strength can be cut back without the American people realizing that unilateral disarmament is the hidden purpose of the tax cut. This Phoenix recommendation was implemented by the tax cut effective January 1, 1964.

Other Phoenix recommendations which have already been put into effect by the Kennedy-Johnson Administration are the "hot line" between the White House and the Kremlin, the cutback in production of nuclear materials, the proposed joint Soviet-U. S. trip to the moon, and U. S. aid to Soviet agriculture.

AESOPIAN LANGUAGE

Since the time of Lenin, the Communists have relayed instructions to Party members by a device known as Aesopian language. Communist plans are described in such a way that certain language will convey an activating message to Party members at the same time that it will allay the fears and deactivate the non-Communists. By this means, Communist bosses can transmit orders through publications which are read by the West.

In the same way, the egghead gravediggers have their own Aesopian lingo. *Foreign Affairs*, the prestige publication of the powerful Council on Foreign Relations, frequently serves the same purpose as the secret documents circulated only in high governmental circles. The gravediggers thus openly publish their plans on the theory that the elite members of the council will read the directions, but that, as always, "the public is too dumb to understand."

In April 1951, *Foreign Affairs* published an article by "Mr. X", later identified as George F. Kennan, which called for abandonment of Eastern Europe to Communism under the disguise of "containment." This plan was faithfully executed by our State Department. The strong but factual

Captive Nations Resolution which Congress directed the President to issue each summer, and which Eisenhower did issue, was watered down by Kennedy and Johnson so as to satisfy the jailor of the captive nations.

Exactly 13 years later, in the April 1964 issue of *Foreign Affairs*, there appeared the article by gravedigger Roswell Gilpatric which announced the plan to end U. S. military supremacy. This is the plan for which the "secret documents" are preparing and brainwashing the American people. This plan will weaken our defenses so much that the Soviets can reduce our "options" to suicide or surrender.

MOTIVES OF THE GRAVEDIGGERS

What is the motive for the gravediggers? Why would American citizens in responsible positions want to disarm America and make us subject to an ultimatum to surrender?

1) The gravediggers sincerely want to put the United States in a world government. They see no hope of Congress or the American people voluntarily voting to repeal the Declaration of Independence. They believe we can be forced into world government as the price of avoiding war with Russia. As a leading gravedigger, Walt W. Rostow, said, we desire "an end to nationhood."[13] Dr. Lincoln P. Bloomfield explained:

> "If the communist dynamic was greatly abated, the west might lose whatever incentive it has for world government."[14]

2) The gravediggers are convinced that Socialism is the wave of the future and they want to be

on the winning side. As Whittaker Chambers said when he left the Communist Party: I felt I was going "from the winning side to the losing side." The gravediggers enjoy their present positions of great power. They believe that by diverting funds from defense into domestic projects that buy votes, they can keep a liberal administration in Washington as long as there is a United States. With no faith in America, they see only the choice of being Red or dead. They do not see that resolute leadership can insure peace through strength.

3) The gravediggers are allied with certain New York financial interests which have been on both sides of many political contests and wars — for financial profit. Averell Harriman's banking group had been granted "a large manganese concession in the Caucasus" by Lenin. Although Communists usually steal foreign investments, Harriman admitted he sold out to Stalin for "a reasonable profit."[15] The gravediggers and their New York backers are opposed to our military, whose training is for patriotism and victory. The Fulbright Memorandum reveals the gravediggers' belief that "most military officers . . . (lack) balance of judgment." The gravediggers waged an unremitting propaganda war against Generals MacArthur, Wedemeyer, Van Fleet and Trudeau, Admirals Burke and Anderson, etc. The gravediggers believe that greater returns can be had if Federal funds are diverted from defense to other projects. Even an inspection system to enforce disarmament would cost more than the price of keeping America strong.

Chapter Eleven

WHO'S LYING NOW?

Arthur Sylvester, Assistant Secretary of Defense for Public Information, stated on December 6, 1962:

> "It's an inherent government right, if necessary, to lie to save itself."

A sample of this lying is the Pentagon's reply to Senator Goldwater's statement of August 19, 1964, that:

> "The nuclear arsenal? Under this Administration, we are facing the decade of the 1970s with the very real prospect of a strategic force capable of carrying only one-tenth of the capacity that can be carried — in the name of peace — today."[1]

The Pentagon replied with this lie to save itself:

> "First, raw megatonnage assigned to strategic forces is a poor measure of military effectiveness, as all informed persons know. A very big bomb that cannot be delivered has no military value. Thus a reduction in our megatonnage would not of itself say anything at all about our real nuclear power."[2]

Senator Goldwater was not speaking about: "a very big bomb that cannot be delivered." He was referring to high-yield nuclear strategic bombs that have been carried by SAC B-52s for many years — and which right now are being carried in the bomb-bays of the airborne alert. These bombs we know by years of actual experience *can be delivered,* and be delivered reliably.

Turning from the slick attempt to deceive by a hanky-panky with confusing words, to the substance of the McNamara contention that megatonnage isn't really important, and that Russian bombs are much too big for practical purposes and tremendously wasteful of power, the conclusive answers are found in two simple scientific formulas or computations. Here is the first:

"A three-fold increase in the explosive power . . . is the same as doubling the number of . . . weapons . . . for the purpose of determining nuclear destructiveness."[3]

Applying the above formula:

1 Khrushchev 100-megaton missile =

66 McNamara 1-megaton missiles in destructive power

The second scientific computation constitutes excerpts from tables prepared by Herman Kahn and the Rand Corporation to indicate the effectiveness of missiles in "lethally damaging" enemy missiles.

EFFECTIVENESS OF AIMED AND AREA ATTACKS[4]

PSI resistance of target	Lethal area (square miles) 1-Megaton	100-Megaton
½	260	5,600
2	90	2,000
10	10	200
25	4	90
100	1.3	30

McNamara contends that there are no *military* targets which require more than 25-megaton warheads for their destruction — thus refusing to recognize that Khrushchev considers the entire population of the United States to be prime military targets, *for which these super-powerful warheads were specifically developed,* and the destruction of which by a genocidal surprise attack will render the U. S. incapable of visiting devastating retaliation against the USSR. McNamara also refuses to recognize the consistently held Soviet doctrine of nuclear targeting, which demands warheads with massive megatonnage. This targeting doctrine was enunciated by Defense Minister Rodion Malinovsky, at the Kremlin, on February 22, 1963, to an audience significantly including military attaches of nations of both East and West:

> "We shall deal a simultaneous blow of several times more missiles [than possessed by the U. S.], and *such a tremendous nuclear yield* that it will wipe off the earth all targets, industrial and administrative-political centers of the United States, will destroy completely the countries which have made available their territories for American war bases."

The Malinovsky threat of U. S. annihilation was made if we should invade Cuba. Khrushchev himself backed up the Malinovsky threat of nuclear war over Cuba in a Moscow speech five days later, on February 27, 1963, extending the protection of a threat of Soviet thermonuclear strikes against the "imperialists" if they should "attack" "any

Soviet state" from Cuba to China, from Viet Nam to East Germany.

Yet McNamara, because he sees no targets upon which he would like to use 100-megaton bombs, still refuses to see that they could serve a very useful purpose indeed for the Soviets. Senator Thomas J. Dodd quoted an expert estimate that it would require only 10 of them to wipe out all our major population centers.

Here is why the Pentagon and McNamara are unable to answer Goldwater's charge that the Johnson Administration is reducing the carrying or delivery capacity of our nuclear weapons to less than 1/10 of what it was under the Eisenhower Administration programs.

Close to 90 percent of our present strategic nuclear striking power — that is, our ability to inflict damage on the enemy — must be delivered by manned bombers. These bombers are capable of carrying about 30 thousand million tons of explosive power. McNamara is scrapping the bombers and relying instead on missiles. His claimed "more than 800 missiles" and 256 Polaris submarine-carried missiles (in 16 submarines, not more than 13 or 14 of which could be in firing position at once) can deliver a total of about 2,000 megatons. But this is only 1/15 of the load that can be delivered by our bombers!

Thus our present claimed nuclear superiority depends on our manned bombers being in existence and being operational.

The Kennedy-Johnson Administration made this claim: "We have enough nuclear power to kill

300,000,000 people in 60 minutes." This statement is deceptive because it does not tell us that such power depends on our striking first, which we will never do — with strategic bombers, which we will soon no longer have. President Kennedy officially declared that we will not strike first, and the Johnson Administration adheres to this doctrine.

Even without a Soviet no-warning surprise attack, however, our claimed nuclear superiority will soon vanish. If Khrushchev can't destroy our bombers, McNamara can. Already he is far advanced in his program of scrapping U. S. bombers. He has killed all programs which call for the replacement of present bombers with advanced-type bombers, and he will not even replace worn-out bombers with new ones of the old type.

Even before his bomber-scrapping is complete, McNamara will have eliminated more than 90 percent of our total nuclear striking power by denying the bombers new advanced weapons such as the Skybolt, which would keep the bombers effective for another five to eight years.

McNamara's program is to cut down our capability from 30 to 40 thousand million tons of explosive power based overwhelmingly on bombers, to 2 to 3 thousand million tons, depending almost exclusively on missiles. The survival of the American people will depend on their understanding these figures.

Here is the box score based upon official U. S. Government programs, Appropriations Acts, and expert testimony, — obviously unbiased because it was given a year before this became a major 1964 political issue:[5]

"From this — as planned by the Eisenhower Administration for the mid-1960s		To this — as planned by the Kennedy Administration for the late 1960s
1,100	B-47 Bombers	0
630	B-52 Bombers	0
80	B-58 Bombers	0
60	Thor Missiles	0
45	Jupiter Missiles	0
126	Atlas Missiles	0
126	Titan Missiles	54
464	Polaris Missiles	656
600	Minuteman Missiles	950+

Nuclear weapons and delivery systems equaling 30-40 billion tons of TNT	Nuclear weapons and delivery systems equaling 2 billion tons of TNT

WHY MANY MILITARY MEN ARE CONCERNED:

In addition to sharp cutback in available U. S. nuclear punch, there is this fact —
No new strategic bomber, missile or space-weapons system is now under serious development for the late 1960s."

Even *Newsweek* concedes that our strategic bombers now have a single strike nuclear yield of 50 thousand megatons in theory, and 30 thousand megatons in practice, and estimates the missile force planned by the Administration for the 1970s as having a delivery potential of only 3,100 megatons.[6]

Whenever McNamara, his Assistant for News-Management Arthur Sylvester, or the anonymous Pentagon spokesmen find that the vast difference in delivery capabilities between missiles and bombers is becoming so apparent that even the most trusting public can no longer be fooled by the slick and shoddy pretext that "megatonnage" is not important, then they fall back on the claim that they never intended to scrap the bombers.

This is utter deceit. The Kennedy-Johnson Administration went into office in January 1961 with pre-prepared plans,[7] discussed with either Khrushchev himself or his direct representative at the 1960 Pugwash Conference,[8] to scrap the U. S. SAC bombers. The first major act of the Administration, under McNamara's "stewardship" of the Pentagon, was to refuse to spend $525 million appropriated by Congress for B-52 bombers.

McNamara then blocked the development of the B-70 as a weapons system, by claiming that the B-52 as modernized by Skybolt missiles, could do the job better and cheaper. Then he killed the Skybolt missile, thus unnecessarily hastening the obsolescense of the B-52s. Between now and 1966 he will have completed the scrapping of 1,400 B-47 bombers.[9] He has recently endorsed the plan proposed by his longtime Deputy Secretary of Defense, Roswell Leavitt Gilpatric, in the Council on Foreign Relations' publication, *Foreign Affairs*[10] which would bring about the total counterforce disarmament of the United States, and scrap both all U. S. bombers, and all U. S. defenses against bombers. He conditioned his endorsement of this plan — not upon any disarmament agreements by the Soviets, but only upon continued appearances of "detente" by them.

Now the Pentagon gravediggers have the gall to pretend they do not intend to scrap the bombers. As soon as the political campaign is over, if they are still in control, the bombers will be scrapped when the public memory fades. Even if they did not "intend" to scrap the bombers, we simply have not built a new strategic bomber of any kind since 1962 — none of the powerful B-52s, none of the supersonic B-58s. Most of the B-52s were delivered far earlier than that — and McNamara froze their greatest total number at 630. The gravediggers claim they will have "large numbers of strategic bombers at every stage" through 1972. At that time, those left will average more than 12 years of age. They will have been deprived of the three greatest aids to their penetration to Soviet targets: (1) hundreds and hundreds of B-47s operating from bases ringing Russia, to clear the way for the B-52s with 10-megaton bombs, and to suppress air defenses; (2) hundreds of U. S. Navy aircraft carrier strategic bombers, to do the same; and (3) the Skybolt missile, which would blast Soviet targets long before the bombers arrived within Soviet air defense reach. By 1966 our B-52s and B-58s will be old and worn out. McNamara froze the B-58 program at a total of 80. Senator Barry Goldwater, a Major General in the U. S. Air Force Reserve, and jet pilot of many years experience, estimates that there may be a total of only about 50 of the two types left by 1970.

Chapter Twelve

McNAMARA'S
MONO-MEGA-MANIA

Your life depends on your understanding just one word. Not only your own life, but the lives of those you love, your fortune, your future, your freedom, and the survival of your country, depend upon the American people being misled no longer as to the meaning of one word. That word represents the greatest power ever known in the world; the only power sufficient to conquer the world, if the Soviets get more of it than we do; the only power sufficient to preserve peace *and* freedom, if we get more of it than they do.

This word represents the decisive factor in every major war of modern times: firepower. In the bygone era of conventional weapons, firepower determined which side would win. In the nuclear age, firepower is vastly more important: *first*, because it is now ten million times greater; *second*, because *winning* a war is no longer good enough. Hundreds of millions of lives, mostly American lives, will be sacrificed if the Soviets launch a nuclear attack against us. Such an attack must be *prevented*, not merely revenged. And only *overwhelming firepower*, possessed by the United States, provides sufficient preventive power to convince the would-be world conqueror that an attack against the United States would doom the entire USSR to utter incineration. Such essential overwhelming firepower is measured, in the terminology of the nuclear age, in MEGATONNAGE.

The American people must learn the meaning of "MEGATONNAGE". A failure to learn in time will permit the fatal disarmament of America.

Strategic nuclear weapons are, as stated by the late President John F. Kennedy, "ten million times more destructive than anything the world has ever known."[1] In World War II, the larger strategic bombs carried 2,000 *pounds* of TNT. "Mega" is the Greek prefix meaning "million". A "megaton", therefore, is the equivalent, in nuclear explosive, of 1 million *tons* of TNT explosive power. "Megatonnage" does not refer to the *weight* of nuclear warheads, but measures their explosive power in terms of TNT. The contrast is quite impressive; it helps to understand the meaning of "megatonnage." In 1961 the total "megatonnage" of the U. S. stockpile of nuclear explosives was authoritatively estimated at 35,000 (that is, 35 kilomegatons), and, it was stated:

> "In the form of TNT this much explosive power would fill a string of freight cars stretching from the earth to the moon and back 15 times."[2]

In the same year, 1961, the Soviet nuclear stockpile was estimated to be 20,000 megatons (20 kilomegatons) — so the U. S. was supreme in megatonnage. But by October of that year, it became clear that Khrushchev had stolen our supremacy through trapping us in Test-Ban I.

Long secret preparations and ban-breaking tests enabled them to get from 5 to 10 times as much explosive power out of each pound of lithium deuteride (the basic H-bomb explosive) by new burning techniques still beyond us. By reworking the material in their 20,000 megaton stockpile with these new techniques, and concentrating on very-high-yield weapons, they could bring it up to between 100,000 and 200,000 megatons of explosive power.

Having been thus duped into losing to the Soviets the advantage of scores of thousands of megatons of strategic power, the Kennedy-Johnson Administration concealed the results of Test-Ban I from the American people[3] so that we would accept the deadly freezing of the U. S. in an inferior position by Test-Ban II[4]. Ever since the gravediggers have been trying to persuade the public that megatonnage is not important, and that a capability of delivering massive megatonnage is not essential to the survival of the United States.

McNamara is scrapping all U. S. massive megatonnage capability.

Khrushchev is building up super-massive megatonnage capability. Are you really willing to have your life staked on McNamara's being right, and Khrushchev's being wrong? Do you really want the survival of your country staked on McNamara's pseudo-sophisticated concept of a strategic "stalemate" — when Khrushchev seeks world-wide victory through overwhelming strategic power? Do you really believe that McNamara's 1-megaton missiles can frighten Khrushchev into abandoning use of his 100-megaton missiles?

Ever since the Kennedy-Johnson Administration took power in 1961, McNamara has been scrapping or blocking development of all U. S. weapons systems capable of delivering warheads of more than 1-megaton. This is the sole common denominator of all his policies and programs relating to strategic weapons: deny to the United States the capability of delivering massive megatonnage on the Soviet Union. People know what he has done to our SAC bombers — past, present, and future; the "cover" for this is that he prefers missiles to bombers — but he is just as much against missiles with massive-megaton warheads as he is against bombers which can deliver massive megatonnage. An authoritative trade journal reported that McNamara's Defense Department had killed 5 out of 6 "study efforts for advanced intercontinental ballistic missiles," and that this "practically brings to a standstill the efforts of the Air Force Ballistic Missiles Division planners to generate ideas and supporting data for ICBMs which could be deployed in the 1970 decade to meet the reasonably expected growth of hostile capabilities."[5]

McNamara also has prevented development of a U. S. capability of delivering massive megatonnage by a large number of small-warheaded missiles, such as Polaris and Minuteman. This is also a key element in the unilateral disarmament campaign designed to provide an "example" to the Soviets. For example, Dr. Harold Brown, Director of Defense Research and Engineering, testified to a House of Representatives Defense Appropriations Subcommittee, on March 11, 1964, that the Pentagon was implementing the policy of "restraint decisions in strategic doctrine." As an example of such "restraints" in the acquisition of weaponry by the U. S., he gave this testimony:

> "On force structure I would say that the decision not to make three or four times as many 'Minuteman' missiles than we are actually making — has probably had an influence on the Soviets."

Asked if that was a unilateral decision on our part, he answered:

> "Yes sir. There were, as you know, proposals to go up to . . . 'Minuteman,' which were not accepted."[6]

McNamara has held down the proposed 1970 total of Minuteman missiles to 1,000. The Air Force requested 2,000. Military experts and strategists have estimated that it would take from 8,000 to 18,000 Minuteman missiles to equal the massive-megatonnage delivery capability of the SAC bombers McNamara is scrapping or has rendered obsolete by cancellation of Skybolt.[7] He has also cut drastically the U. S. numbers of strategic weapons delivery capability, and also the essential delivery system "mix", by stripping the U. S. Navy aircraft carriers of their strategic bombing capability.

In contrast to McNamara's apparent emotional monomania against weapons of massive megatonnage, Khrushchev has a coldly-calculating dedication to nuclear super-weapons. He thinks the world of them, because they alone can provide him with the power sufficient to conquer the world, through a surprise genocidal attack on the United States. In 1957, some four years before the Kennedy-Johnson Administration came into power with its pre-prepared plan to scrap all U. S. first-strike and massive megatonnage delivery capability, Khrushchev began his big, secret buildup to produce nuclear super-weapons. He concentrated the total resources of the USSR in science, technology, and industry, on three phases of weapons development.

Khrushchev demanded of his nuclear scientists missile warheads tremendously more powerful out of the same weight of explosive material. He got them. Little wonder that he declared, in 1961, "We would be slobbering idiots not to carry out the nuclear tests."[8]

Khrushchev demanded of his rocket scientists and technologists, missiles which could carry pay loads four times greater than U. S. missiles — and he got those, too. Despite misleading statements about U. S. space accomplishments, the Soviets are still as far ahead of us in military rocket payload capacity as they were in 1957, when Senator Lyndon B. Johnson made his investigations of U. S. space and preparedness programs.[9]

Khrushchev's third demand on his scientists was for delivery vehicles which could flank the U. S. warning nets, and thus provide a no-warning spearhead for his genocidal surprise attack, which could destroy on the ground the U. S. SAC bomb-

ers which McNamara had not yet been able to
scrap. Again, he secured what he needed to carry
out his plan. The Soviets now have submarines
which can carry powerful strategic nuclear missiles, with a 500 mile range permitting them to
cover all of the great U. S. coastal targets. And
they have now also missiles capable of delivering
the nuclear warheads over the *South* Pole — and
we are caught with all of our warning nets facing
north. About half of our SAC bombers can get
off safely with 15 minutes warning from their
alert status — but such systems as Khrushchev now
has will give far less warning than 15 minutes.

These, then are the facts of the contrasting U. S.
and USSR strategic military programs. They are
developing ever more powerful warheads and massive capabilities for delivery, whereas McNamara
is cutting ours down to a limit of little more than
1-megaton per delivery vehicle.

Chapter Thirteen

A NUCLEAR PEARL HARBOR?

As Khrushchev surveys the world situation in 1964, the facts force him to these conclusions. Peaceful competition with the West has reached a dead-end. As Victor Riesel reported: "Khrushchev's economy is not cracking — it has cracked." Soviet agriculture is incapable of feeding the people. The Russian people have less beef and less housing than they had under the Czars. The Soviet industrial system cannot produce sufficient capital or consumer goods.[1]

As a realistic Khrushchev surveys the satellites, he sees the same economic failure. Hungary, which was once "a Canaan of milk and honey," is today a land of starving people where slaughtering a calf or pig without permission brings twice the prison sentence of first-degree murder. Unprecedented shortages of food and other essentials in Cuba make it terribly expensive to keep the props under Castro.

Even after being bailed out with the American wheat deal of December, 1963, the Soviet economic position is deteriorating rapidly. All the world now knows the vivid contrast between Communist East Germany and capitalist West Germany, and soon the world will know the economic failure of the entire Socialist system. A continuation of peaceful competition with the West can result only in the Communists losing their position of world leadership.

How then can Khrushchev hope to achieve his goal of global conquest? Only by the elimination of the United States, which would make inevitable the collapse of the Free World and enable the USSR to maintain dominance over a dynamic Communist movement.

As Khrushchev searches for the solution to this problem and the fulfillment of his fondest hope, he is not restricted by any religious, moral, patriotic or humanitarian bonds. The "Butcher of Budapest" and the "Hangman of the Ukraine" is not hampered by our code of civilized conduct.

RED DOCTRINE ON WAR

History shows that Communists believe in surprise attacks on their victims. This was the way the Communists attacked Poland, Finland, Japanese Manchuria, and South Korea. Captain Nikolai Artamanov, a career officer of the Soviet Navy, testified before the U. S. House Committee on Un-American Activities:

> "Since February, 1955, Soviet strategy has been based on the doctrine of surprise attack in nuclear warfare."[2]

This is confirmed by the current views of top Soviet officers on the advantages of the nuclear first-strike, published in a symposium called *Military Strategy* edited by Marshal V. D. Sokolovskii.[3]

The Communists know that Americans are a trusting people; we ignored all the pre-Pearl Harbor evidence of Japanese intentions provided by decoding their messages and by House Committee on Un-American Activities reports on Japanese espionage.

The repeat murderer does not challenge his next victim to a duel. He stalks his prey and assassinates him at the opportune moment. Assassination has always been a prime tactic of the Communists. They don't give up after they pick a target. The world Communist apparatus spent many years of careful planning to eliminate Trotsky in Mexico City and Krivitsky in a Washington, D. C. hotel.

When the Communists have had sufficient power, they have not contented themselves with mere conquest of a country, they have pushed their victory to the limits of genocide, of decimation of the nation, or at least of its leaders. The stark facts of Soviet conquest in Poland, the Baltic States and some of the separate nations within the USSR, and of Chinese Red conquest of Tibet, prove that the Communists believe in and carry out a planned liquidation of every leader and potential leader.[4]

Communist doctrine seeks to avoid "waging" a nuclear "war," but has no inhibitions against the assassination or the extermination of its enemy. Strategic nuclear weapons, of the warhead power developed only by the Soviets, now for the first time in history make possible the "assassination" of an entire nation.

This means that Khrushchev comes to the logical conclusion that the nuclear destruction of the United States of America is his best and final step to world conquest. Annihilation of our population would be the most reliable means of eliminating the United States. Khrushchev's nuclear super-weapons can be adapted to the Strategy of Genocide with little risk of U. S. retaliation or of substantial damage to the USSR.

If Khrushchev's surprise first-strike is of sufficient magnitude, we will have lost substantially our entire population and be incapable, both physically and rationally, of "waging" any kind of war. We would probably be incapable of making any effective retaliation.

RED PASSION FOR "PLANS"

This objective is so clear, and its execution is so simple, that it fits in perfectly with Communist military-political thinking. The Soviets must have a "plan" for a sure win in the great and decisive contest with the United States. The fundamental ideology of Communism demands a "plan" for everything. It is a "planned" society, with a "planned" economy, a "planned" system of agriculture, a "planned" system of education, even a "plan" to control family relationships.

Likewise, the Communists have had a brilliant "plan" to achieve a sure-win in each of the "small" wars we have waged. By a combination of bluff in Moscow and "opinion subversion" in Washington, the Reds have duped us into conducting "small" wars according to rules they lay down for us — but do not follow themselves.

In Korea they made us respect the "privileged sanctuary", and also agree to "negotiations" when it was to the Reds' advantage instead of ours. At the Bay of Pigs, we were reminded of the rule against "intervention" just in time to cause us to

break our pledge of air support which would have
brought victory to the Cuban Freedom Fighters.
In Laos, the threat of "escalation" led us to abandon the anti-Communist forces we had promised
to defend. In South Viet Nam, the Reds require
us to abide by the Geneva Accords which were
never followed by the Communists.

And in all these "small" wars, we would tremble
even to think of violating the number-one rule
prescribed for us by Communist propaganda: that
the U. S., would be "insane" to use even the
smallest, cleanest nuclear tactical weapon — even
if it would shorten a war by years, bring a victory
to our side, and save thousands of American lives.

A Soviet leadership, brilliant enough to con-
ceive such plans for sure-wins in "small" wars,
would not leave to chance the outcome of the
contest for control of the world. Knowledge of
Communist history, objectives and tactics warns
us that there must be a "plan" — designed to complete conquest of the world with the highest de-
gree of certainty and in the shortest practical
time.[5]

The ideal preparation for the Strategy of Genocide would be a dramatic reduction in U. S.
military strength brought about by U. S. unilateral
disarmament. Even without such a drastic advance reduction, the Strategy of Genocide would
still make sense if the "no warning" Soviet surprise
strike could take out enough of the alert U. S.
strategic capabilities. This would be followed by
an immediate massive attack which would wipe
out the remainder of our capabilities, plus our

communication and command system, so that any retaliatory attack by us would be quite limited.

Only the weapons of his "no-warning" attack need outflank our early warning system. They can come over Antarctica, from submarines, from Cuba, or from cannisters concealed underwater off our coasts. The weapons to annihilate us could be launched from Soviet territory and would not be impeded substantially by even an hour's warning.

Khrushchev thus has a good chance to gain the world by the expenditure of only a few hundred strategic missiles. He need not even replace the missiles he uses, since once the United States is wiped out, what little nation would dare to defy the Communist colossus?

RISKING NUCLEAR WAR

Now assume that U. S. Intelligence discovered the massive Soviet buildup for a genocidal surprise attack. Assume further that the U. S. leadership recognized the threat of the Soviet secret first-strike missile program to be as great or greater than when Soviet first-strike strategic missiles were secretly placed in Cuba in 1962. Experience and logic tell us that, if the Johnson Administration is still in power, this is what we can expect:

We would send Averell Harriman to Moscow to request more disarmament negotiations with the Soviets. McNamara would speed up the dismantling of our military strength and give up more bases in order to "show our good faith." The President would issue conciliatory statements in order to "ease tensions," and possibly even invite Khrushchev to Washington. Adlai Stevenson would tell the United Nations to decide whether or not the U. S. has the right to protect itself.

Is this fantastic? Yes, but no more so than the reaction of the Kennedy-Johnson Administration to past Soviet threats to destroy us. Our reaction to the Soviet betrayal in 1961 of the first Nuclear Test Ban was *not* to try to regain the supremacy we had lost, but to engage in more test-ban negotiations to guarantee permanence of Soviet supremacy. The reaction of the Kennedy-Johnson Administration to the Cuban missile threat was to start scrapping the SAC and Navy strategic nuclear bombers — which composed 90 percent of the U. S. ability to meet the Soviet threat. In the climactic days of the crisis, our number-one request was for more disarmament negotiations and a second test ban.

The best way of judging what the Johnson Administration will do in the future is to look at the past record. We can only conclude that, at whatever level of strategic capability a Soviet first-strike missile buildup should catch us, the most probable reaction of the Johnson Administration would be to disarm immediately and drastically. The first to go would be any U. S. nuclear weapons which, like our strategic bombers, are superior to anything the Reds have.

After America is disarmed, it is possible that the Soviets, instead of launching a surprise first-strike, would give us an ultimatum for surrender by total disarmament. What would we do then? The most likely result would be a U. S. surrender disguised as a purported bilateral disarmament arrangement in which we merely took the "initiative."

The Administration could put this over by "managed news" and bureaucratic doubletalk. The Roosevelt Administration presented the Yalta sellout as "One of the most important steps ever taken to promote peace and happiness in the world".[6] *The New York Times, Time, Life* and most of the news media joined in lavish praise of Yalta as "a great achievement."[7]

The Kennedy-Johnson Administration presented the Cuban crisis to the American people as a great victory and as evidence that we had made Khrushchev back down! — whereas the truth is that the deal was a defeat for the U. S., binding us to give up our bases in Turkey and Italy, guarantee Castro against any invasion, and accept Khrushchev's word on how many missiles he withdrew. We still don't know whether any missiles left the island or are stored in Cuba's numerous caves. Chester Bowles and other Administration spokesmen even refer to the Laos and Viet Nam retreats as "victories."

Khrushchev has several reasons for believing there is a good chance that the United States will not retaliate against his surprise first-strike.

First, he is convinced that the present U. S. leadership is "too liberal to fight" — even for vital interests. Khrushchev knows that U. S. liberals have convinced themselves that nuclear war is the most terrible evil of all — more terrible than the Red firing squads which dropped Poles in mass graves, more terrible than the slow genocide practiced on nations from Eastern Europe to Tibet —

in other words, "rather Red than dead." He knows that "opinion subversion," Red slogans and propaganda have seriously underminded the American will to resist.

Secondly, Khrushchev knows that the U. S. gravediggers have so substantially disarmed America that our one-time supremacy is already gone. He knows that the plans of Nitze, Gilpatric, Rostow, Weisner, and the Pugwashers are not faint hopes for the future — but present reality under McNamara's disarmament program. He knows that the McNamara Gap has given the Soviets the opening Communism has waited for since Lenin.

Khrushchev's third reason for estimating that the Soviets may get off scot-free after striking the U. S. (or have much less damage than Russia sustained in World War II) is the enormous power of the super weapons he has already tested. They can at the same time knock out a large proportion of all U. S. weapons systems, *and* our communications, command and control systems, *plus* the people who have the authority to order retaliation.

While the Kennedy-Johnson Administration disarms, the Soviets are continuing to build the most powerful missiles with their vastly superior technology in the high-yield areas (thanks to Test Ban I and Test Ban II). The most recent series of Soviet surface-to-surface missiles are at least twice as powerful as their immediate predecessors.

The Soviets are exploiting their superior rocket thrust to develop missiles capable of delivery over the South Pole. This is what Khrushchev meant when he expressed his admiration for his new missile which, "while you were waiting for it at the front door, would be climbing in the back window." The South Pole missile is obviously designed solely for the no-warning spearhead of a surprise attack, since our ballistic missile early warning nets are oriented north.

In every way, the Soviets are concentrating on the highest possible yield strategic missiles — ideally suited for knocking out our Minuteman missiles and destroying substantially our total population. Furthermore, there is no indication whatsoever that the Soviets are going to pile any of their growing bomber fleet on Dean Rusk's "bomber bonfire." Armed with bombs of up to 160 megatons, Khrushchev's bombers would have a free-ride over the U. S. after a surprise missile attack.

The U. S. does not know now — and because of the Moscow Nuclear Test Ban Treaty cannot hope to find out — what maximum effect the explosion of 100+ megaton bombs will have on our Minuteman missile system. We do know that our Minutemen are vulnerable to such missiles, and that a single Soviet missile might take out more than one of ours. Under the McNamara program, these missiles will soon make up the vast majority of our deliverable strategic weapons. Considering the accuracy and high-yield of the many Soviet weapons, it is probable that many of our weapons could be knocked out by shock, or have their circuits fused by the electromagnetic pulse effect, or in other yet unknown fashion.

The Soviet surprise first-strike could give us a

communications problem that we could not solve. This would apply even to communications with Polaris submarines on station. The Chief of Naval Operations has indicated the possibility of very high-yield explosions blacking out communications for hundreds of miles by the electromagnetic pulse effect.

Then, of course, there is the question of who would be left alive with authority and facilities to give the "fire" order. The complicated precautions we have already taken against "accidental" war have greatly hamstrung our ability to give and execute the "fire" order in a real war.

Khrushchev's fourth reason for estimating that the Soviets could come off scot-free is one he could plan for in advance. In making his surprise first-strike against the U. S., he could spare a large area and part of our population so as to follow up with the weapon of blackmail. If Khrushchev carefully calculated his surprise first-strike to wipe out 50 or 100 million Americans, those remaining would be well convinced that he could finish the job and that resistance was useless. This would take care of our Polaris submarines, a number of which might be expected to survive the strike.

Some Americans argue that the Communists do not want to destroy the United States because they want to conquer us intact and enjoy the benefits of our real estate and industries. But if, to win the world, Khrushchev had to pay the price of wiping out American cities, the Soviets would still gain about 10 first-class cities — in good working order — for each of their own destroyed by any blunted

U. S. retaliation. Housing is better in all the cities they would take over, the climate is apt to be much better, the state of industrialization higher.

What do Russian cities have that Russians can't obtain better in Rome, Paris, London, Brussels, Antwerp, West Berlin, Cologne, Venice, Naples, Tokyo — and Geneva? Not even the historic neutrals could hope to stand against the Soviet monopoly of nuclear weapons, strategic and tactical.

KHRUSHCHEV'S ALTERNATIVE

If Khrushchev does not launch the surprise first-strike, what does the future hold for him? In all the decisive "peaceful" contests, the Communists will be defeated by the United States, Western Europe and Japan. Losing the agricultural and industrial production races will seal the fate of Communism as a system. At every break in the Iron and Bamboo Curtains, the people are voting with their feet; they are climbing over barbed-wire fences, running across mined fields, and jumping out of second-story windows to escape from Communism. No one is running the other way. The peoples of all nations, including Russia, will see that the Communist system cannot compete. Soviet leadership, having failed to win the competition with the free world, may be supplanted by the Chinese Red leadership.

In this case, Khrushchev would be left as the leader of the losing side. This lends life-or-death significance to a recent statement by Khrushchev. In a rare moment of truth, he expressed doubt that an agreement banning the use of nuclear weapons in war would be effective. He told Lord

Thompson in Kazakhstan:

> "The trouble is the *losing side will always use nuclear weapons in the last resort to avoid defeat*. If a man thinks he's going to die he'll take any steps."[8] (Emphasis added).

This has a deadly double application. It could mean that *if Khrushchev is losing* the cold war, he will resort to nuclear weapons to turn defeat into victory. On the other hand, if he thinks *we are losing*, he will be convinced that before his final victory, *we* would "use nuclear weapons in the last resort to avoid defeat," so he would launch his preventive strike to destroy the United States and thus avert the destruction of the USSR.

Either way, if the Soviets do launch their surprise nuclear first-strike against the U. S., they will apparently solve all their most critical internal and external problems. By striking us, the Soviets will eliminate the free-enterprise competition with which they cannot live. Speaking to a joint session of the Supreme Soviet, Khrushchev said:

> "We are competing with the capitalist world, and especially with the United States. We shall win without fail."

Wagging a finger at foreign newsmen in the upper gallery of the Kremlin Hall where the Soviet parliament was meeting, he declared in an off-the-cuff taunt:

> "To those gentlemen correspondents who are smiling, let me say, 'People who laugh last, laugh best'."[9]

Khrushchev probably does believe that, if he eliminated U. S. competition, the Communist system would indeed work — and he would have the last laugh. The huge Soviet investment in strategic armaments could be turned to other lines since only smaller weapons would be needed to keep order in the Communist one-world. The destruction of the United States by the Soviet Union would provide the "object lesson" necessary to impose Soviet discipline on the world. Even the farmers and industrial workers might produce more efficiently, if they knew there was never to be an alternative.

If Khrushchev fails to strike, he forfeits his objective of world conquest. If he waits, he may lose even the satellites. His great investment in wresting from the United States supremacy in the technology of the decisive types of nuclear superweapons will have been in vain. Communists everywhere will scorn him as a timid leader who was afraid to press the button which would bring quick victory.

Khrushchev is now 70. In 1960 at Kaprun, Austria, he said:

> "In the short time I still have to live, I would like to see the day when the Communist flag flies over the whole world."[10]

Time, U. S. disarmament, Soviet military strategy, and his own thinking combine to tell Khrushchev that a surprise nuclear attack on the United States is his best way to fly the Communist flag over the whole world. Our danger is not from "accidental" war, but from a deliberate surprise attack.

Chapter Fourteen

OUR CHOICE — WITH NO SECOND CHANCE

In 1964, the American people have a clear choice between "rather Red than dead" and "better ready than dead." On the one hand, we can take a phony "peace" through accommodation and disarmament — which will lead inevitably to a nuclear Pearl Harbor or surrender. On the other hand, we can choose peace *and* freedom through preparedness.

The issue is survival. If our choice is wrong, there will be no second chance.

Most Americans still do not realize how close we came to nuclear destruction two years ago. This danger was pictured vividly by the head of the U. S. Marine Corps, General David M. Shoup, when he made his official report on New Year's Day, 1963. General Shoup began his message with these words:

> "Only by the grace of God and an aerial photograph am I able to address many of you today in person instead of your spirits."

In other words, "only by the grace of God and an aerial photograph" was our country saved from nuclear destruction in October, 1962.

This was confirmed by a highly-authentic column written by a newspaperman who was a close personal friend of President Kennedy, Joseph Alsop. This column stated:

> "Even today remarkably few people have grasped what a horrendously narrow squeak the United States had in the Cuban affair in October, 1962."

Alsop's documented column shows that the U-2 flight which finally — and in the last desperate measure of time — revealed the presence of Soviet offensive missiles in Cuba, would not have been made without heavy public and political pressure on the Administration. The very first flight after the U-2 flights were restored, revealed the presence of offensive missiles, zeroed in on U. S. targets — and revealed them just in time.

This is what General Shoup meant when he said we were saved from nuclear destruction by an aerial photograph. When the missiles were discovered, we destroyed the element of surprise and Khrushchev was willing to pull them out and wait until he could catch us off guard again.

Cuba in October 1962 was a nuclear Pearl Harbor that almost happened. It was much more. It set the stage for a nuclear Pearl Harbor that will happen next year, or perhaps the year after, if we do not stop our futile attempts to make our national security depend on Soviet promises and on such myths as "it's safer to be weak than strong."

On October 9, 1962, FBI Director J. Edgar Hoover, in speaking to the National Convention of the American Legion, gave this advice:

> "A 'soft' approach toward the menace of Communism can lead only to national dis-

aster. . . . We cannot defeat Communism with Socialism, nor with secularism, nor with pacifism, nor with appeasement or accommodation. . . . The fight against crime and Communism can be won, and it will be won with, but only with the help of every decent American citizen."

American citizens are forever asking the question: "But what can just one individual do?" Every American citizen who participated in the public clamor to do something about Cuba in October of 1962 rendered a service to our country. Those thousands of citizens in every state truly saved America from a nuclear Pearl Harbor by forcing the Kennedy-Johnson Administration to restore the U-2 flights over Cuba.

What can these American citizens do now to prevent the nuclear Pearl Harbor that may happen next year, or the year after? Inform your fellow Americans of the facts of our choice in 1964 — with no second chance. A massive campaign of managed news is deliberately concealing from the American people the truth about this choice.

Military weakness has involved us in shooting wars four times in the last 37 years: under President Wilson in 1917, under President Roosevelt in 1941, under President Truman in Korea, and under President Kennedy in Viet Nam. Twice our weakness caused the enemy to launch sneak, surprise attacks on our positions.

Lyndon Johnson is making strenuous efforts in his 1964 political campaign to picture himself in the image of a "middle of the road" candidate.

Every time he opens his mouth on nuclear weapons, however, his reckless words mark him as a man who would lead us to the end of the road for America. For political purposes, he seeks to capitalize on the sincere longing of the people for "peace" — and says things which lead our ruthless enemy to believe we will no longer defend peace and freedom. This invites nuclear war.

A careful examination of Lyndon Johnson's campaign speeches shows that it is really LBJ who is risking nuclear war by "shooting from the lip":

1) LBJ's loose talk in Detroit stripped the effectiveness of the joint U. S.-NATO shield against Soviet invasion of Western Europe. Up to now the Soviets have been deterred from attack because they believed the U. S. had the courage and common sense to use small but powerful tactical nuclear weapons to save the lives of thousands of soldiers. President Kennedy declared that we had "calmly resolved" to use nuclear weapons if necessary to protect the freedom of West Berlin. But LBJ, in his Detroit Labor Day speech, retreated from this position. He told the Reds we fear that if we use even small nuclear weapons, it will cost us 100 million lives, our cities, farms and industry.[1]

Our arsenal of some 25,000 small tactical nuclear weapons constituted the chief practical defense of Western Europe. Because their deterrence factor is their chief value — rather than their use—Johnson's "shooting from the lip" wiped out their primary effectiveness faster than Khrushchev could have done it.

2) No national leader since the world began has made such a reckless statement as Johnson's repeated declaration that today "general war is impossible." David Lawrence in *U. S. News & World Report* revealed the danger in this LBJ statement, under the headline "One Way to Bring On the War That Nobody Wants," showing that the "image of a nation paralyzed with fear of nuclear conflict . . irresoluteness, defeatism" could be misunderstood by the Soviets and bring on war.

Even giving the Johnson statement the benefit of the *Newsweek* interpretation, and translating "general war is impossible" into "unthinkable," distinguished expert opinion believes that this could cause "the most catastrophic mistake in history," and gives the aggressor "the capability for staging an unlimited number of Munichs" — or even an "Armageddon."[2]

3) The Cuban missile crisis of 1962 shows us what it means to have Johnson's finger on the trigger. Long before the Soviets sneaked their "offensive" missiles into Cuba in the fall of 1962, there was a proposal to use American seapower to put a peaceful quarantine around Cuba to turn back as "contraband" all foreign weapons and war materials. If this common-sense action had been taken, the Soviets could never have moved their missiles to Cuba and thereby posed a deadly threat to our nation later averted only "by the grace of God and an aerial photograph."

But LBJ opposed the peaceful quarantine proposal and "intoned that a blockade was an act of war."[3] When the blockade was finally put on, the

Soviets did *not* treat it as an "act of war" — but it was too little and too late to accomplish what could have been done had that resolute action not been blocked. To blockade Cuba before the missiles went in would have been a great decision — if made in time. Because it was too late, it only locked the door after the missiles were already there.

At certain climactic times in history, there is such a thing as the irreplaceable man. One of these was General George Washington. He was not one of the initiators of the Revolution. Jefferson, Madison and Hamilton easily surpassed him in intellect. But Washington had the strength of character to get the job done, and the leadership to inspire others to follow him.

Such a man was General Douglas MacArthur. Without him, Japan would have been handed over to the Communists, setting ahead their timetable by a score of years. Because of her industrial plants, Japan had much higher priority on the Communist takeover list than China. Only MacArthur had the fortitude and the intelligence to balk Communist and State Department plans for Japan.

In 1964, General Barry Goldwater is the irreplaceable man. Only he has the knowledge of the danger we are in because of the McNamara Gap, and the political prestige to do anything about it. Only he has the strength and the leadership to turn the gravediggers out of office. Only he can give us PEACE WITHOUT SURRENDER.

Barry Goldwater knows that American military

and nuclear power is the last best hope of the free world — and indeed our only hope of ensuring "the blessings of liberty to ourselves and our posterity." He knows that the sage advice given us by the Father of our Country is our best maxim today:

> "If we desire to secure peace . . . it must be known that we are at all times ready for war."

If elected President, we can be confident that Goldwater would close the McNamara Gap, wash out the Pugwashers, and break up the Nitze Axis. He would stop the scrapping of present bombers and develop powerful new aerospace weapons systems. He would reconstitute and modernize SAC. He would redouble our airborne alert force and maintain it. He would increase the power of our strategic warheads, step up the production rate and number of missiles. He promises us:

> "I pledge from the depths of my heart and conscience that as President of this nation I would consider it my foremost duty to keep the peace and to keep freedom at the same time. . . . I pledge that the immediate and full restoration of our defense would be one of my first acts as President of the United States."

History teaches us that resolute firmness and prompt decisions make the Reds back down every time. In 1958 when the Chinese Reds tried to capture Quemoy and Matsu, and all the liberals cried "Why die for Quemoy?", President Eisenhower went on television and told the world the U. S. would stand firm in the Formosa Straits. Within a week the Reds backed down — and these off-shore islands are still free.

Wise young aviators have a saying: "I don't want to be the 'hottest' pilot — just the oldest." To become the oldest pilot requires a career of life-or-death decisions, made prudently and promptly. There is no margin for error, for reckless acts, or late decisions. Barry Goldwater — one of America's oldest jet pilots — would be the safest, surest hand to have on our nuclear trigger. He has the qualities which count: courage and competence, and integrity. Most Americans would rather entrust their lives to a prudent pilot than a dangerous driver (90 MPH!).

In the meantime, for the survival of our nation, Americans should raise nationwide protest to persuade Lyndon Johnson to do the very things Goldwater would do naturally, enthusiastically and more competently. An aroused public opinion should make the gravediggers more of a political liability than Bobby Baker. We must have a full-scale Congressional investigation of the gravediggers in the State Department, the Pentagon, the CIA, the White House staff and the Disarmament Agency.

Pride is number one on most theologians' list of sins. It was pride which caused Lucifer to tell God he would not serve. It was pride which caused Adam and Eve to disobey God and thereby lose Paradise. If we lose our beloved America, the nearest thing to Paradise on earth, it will be because of pride. Too many of what J. Edgar Hoover called the "decent American citizens" are ignoring the obvious warnings because they are too comfortable in their prosperity, and too confident that America can never lose. They have fallen victim to the cleverest Communist slogan of them all: "It can't happen here."

Every country taken over by the Communists had the best people thinking, "it can't happen here." Newspaperman George Sokolsky told of being in Russia in the months before the Bolsheviks took over, and how the businessmen and nobility stood around at their parties and laughed at the "parlor pinks" as a harmless, ragged bunch. Within a few months, all those who laughed were dead or in exile.

Father James Keller of the Christophers published a letter from a young Czech which describes how that once prosperous, democratic nation slipped behind the Iron Curtain:

> "Everybody took it for granted that because we were a freedom-loving people, we could never lose freedom. We paid no attention to repeated warnings that the Communists were infiltrating into the heart of everything that affected our destiny. The majority of us went on living in our smug little worlds, too busy with business, parties, ski trips, and the rest to realize the frightful penalty we were soon to pay for our neglect. One morning our bitter fate came upon us like a shot out of hell. We were helpless to do anything about it. Machine guns lined the streets. The Government, the Army, the Schools, communications, — everything had been taken over by

the Communists overnight. Will we ever get
another chance?"

When the Communists pushed their drive to
take over China, the pundits and commentators
told us this was impossible. China had no capitalism, and Marx had said Communism would
only win in countries with capitalistic abuses. The
sanctity of the family and ancestor worship were
the strongest factors in Chinese life, and such a
people would never accept Communism. Besides,
the Chinese have always "absorbed their conquer-
ors." Twenty million liquidations later, the Chinese have absorbed only tyranny and tragedy.

Then there was Cuba. We were told, it couldn't
possibly happen there! The Monroe Doctrine and
the U. S. Navy would prevent any Communist
conquest of Cuba. Anyway, the Latins are far too
volatile ever to be regimented by Communist discipline. But Cuba is a Communist island today.

We must not let the sin of pride tell us "it can't
happen here." It can happen here, and it will happen here — via a nuclear Pearl Harbor, or a surrender ultimatum — unless "decent American citizens" take immediate and vigorous steps to protect
our lives and freedom — not only against the
enemy who has vowed to "bury" us, but against
the U. S. gravediggers who are preparing our
graves — who disarm us while the enemy arms
100-million fold.

The voters must choose: War from weakness,
or peace through strength; suicide through surrendering our arms, or survival in freedom.

REFERENCES

Chapter 1: Who Will Bury Us?

1. Lenin, *Selected Works*, Vol. VII, p. 298.
2. *U. S. News & World Report*, Dec. 27, 1957, p. 32.
3. *Time*, Sept. 21, 1962, p. 17.
4. Speech in Springfield, Ill., Jan. 27, 1837.

Chapter 2: The Biggest Gyp in History

1. *St. Louis Post-Dispatch*, Sept. 10, 1962.

Chapter 3: The McNamara Gap

1. American Security Council, *Washington Report*, June 29, 1964; "Is U. S. Giving Up in Arms Race?", *U. S. News & World Report*, Aug. 5, 1963, pp. 37-43; "Worry Over U. S. Defense: A 'Maginot Line' of Missiles?", *U. S. News & World Report*, Mar. 9, 1964, pp. 38-41.
2. *Look Magazine*, Aug. 25, 1964, p. 17; *U. S. News & World Report*, Aug. 24, 1964, p. 20.
3. *U. S. News & World Report*, Aug. 5, 1963, p. 38; Craig Hosmer, Member of Joint Congressional Committee on Atomic Energy in *Washington Report*, May 11, 1964.
4. *St. Louis Post-Dispatch*, Aug. 30, 1964, p. 4A.
5. Address to Commonwealth Club of California, San Francisco, Dec. 7, 1962.
6. Fourth Successful Missile Intercept Kwajalein Island dispatch Apr. 5, 1963; First Successful Test, *New York Times*, Nov. 16, 1961.
7. *New York Times*, Aug. 13, 1964; Dispatch from Washington, Aug. 12, by John W. Finney.
8. *Aviation Week & Space Technology*, Mar. 16, 1964, p. 84; Id. p. 79.
9. Statement by Robert S. McNamara to Democratic Platform Committee, *New York Times*, Aug. 18, 1964, p. 18.

Chapter 4: Our Enemy's Secret Weapon

1. Lenin, *Selected Works*, Vol. VII, p. 298.
2. Article by J. Edgar Hoover, guest columnist for Victor Riesel's syndicated column, *St. Louis Globe-Democrat*, July 20, 1962.
3. Hoover, J. Edgar, "The Crime of the Century," *Reader's Digest*, May 1951, p. 149.
4. Patterns of Communist Espionage, report of the House Committee on Un-American Activities, Jan. 1959, pp. 78-79.
5. "The Double Cross That Gave the Reds the H-Bomb," *Look*, July 13, 1953, p. 24.
6. Zacharias, R. Adm. Ellis M., "The Atom Spy Who Got Away," *Real Magazine*, July 1953, p. 7.
7. *The Net That Covers The World* by E. H. Cookridge, p. 87.
8. *Soviet Atomic Espionage*, Joint Committee on Atomic Energy, Government Printing Office, 1951, p. 183.
9. *Soviet Atomic Espionage*, p. 181.
10. Ibid.
11. Senate Internal Security Subcommittee hearing, May 7, 1953.
12. *Report of the Canadian Royal Commission*, June 27, 1946, p. 449.
13. *Expose of Soviet Espionage* by J. Edgar Hoover to the Senate Judiciary Committee, May, 1960, pp. 29-30.
14. *Secret War for the A-Bomb* by Dr. Medford Evans, p. 50.
15. "Spy Permitted to Escape With A-Bomb Secrets," *Chicago Tribune*, Aug. 22, 1953.
16. *Coronet Magazine*, March, 1953, p. 89.
17. *The Secret War for the A-Bomb*, p. 169.

18. Department of State Publication 2498, Government Printing Office, 1946.
19. Speech to Senate, April 2, 1947.
20. *New York Times,* Feb. 16, 1946.
21. *The Secret War for the A-Bomb,* p. 230.
22. DeToledano, Ralph, *The Greatest Plot in History,* Duell, Sloan & Pearce, N. Y.
23. Bulletin Atomic Scientists, Jan., 1947.
24. *U. S. News & World Report,* June 25, 1954, p. 79-80; June 11, 1954, p. 82ff.
25. *East Minus West=Zero* by Dr. Werner Keller, pp. 323-330.

Chapter 5: Suckers for Slogans

1. Kissinger, Dr. Henry A., *Nuclear Weapons and Foreign Policy.*
2. Davies, Joseph, *Mission to Moscow.*
3. *The Fortress That Never Was* by Rodney G. Minot; also Walter Trohan's column in the *Chicago Tribune,* Aug. 15, 1964.
4. Khrushchev, N. S., "For New Victories for the World Communist Movement," *World Marxist Review,* Jan., 1961.
5. *The Worker,* Midwest Edition, Apr. 29, 1962.
6. *The Worker,* Feb. 18, 1964, p. 5.
7. Hook, Sidney, *The Fail-Safe Fallacy,* Stein-Day; Mallan, Lloyd, *Peace is a Three Edged-Sword,* Prentice-Hall.
8. Teller, Dr. Edward and Latter, Albert L., *Our Nuclear Future: Facts, Dangers, and Opportunities,* Criterion.
9. *Reader's Digest,* May 1962, p. 49.
10. Limpus, Lowell, *Disarm,* Freedom Press.
11. *Reader's Digest,* May 1964, p. 75.
12. Address to Congress, Jan. 8, 1790.

Chapter 6: The Nitze Axis

1. *Power and Policy Problems in the Defense of the West,* by Paul H. Nitze, Asilomar *Proceedings.*
2. Ibid., p. 9.
3. *Foreign Affairs,* April, 1964, p. 355, 356, 358.
4. Ibid., p. 373-374.
5. Ibid., p. 368.

Chapter 7: Pugwash Brainwash

1. U. S. Senate Internal Security Subcommittee, *The Pugwash Conferences,* 1961, p. 28.
2. Rostow, Walt W., *"The Long Run and the Short Run,"* Sixth Pugwash Conference, Dec. 5, 1960.
3. *Human Events,* Aug. 10, 1963, p. 8.
4. American Security Council, *Washington Report,* July 6, 1964.
5. Interview with McNamara, *Saturday Evening Post,* Dec. 1, 1962, p. 18.

Chapter 8: Far to the Left of Even Humphrey

1. Department of State Publication 7277, pp. 3-4.
2. *Human Events,* Apr. 14, 1962.
3. U. S. Arms Control & Disarmament Agency, Contract Report of Peace Research Institute.
4. Burnham, James, *Suicide of the West,* John Day Co., N. Y.

Chapter 9: Crawling to Moscow

1. Position Paper of Joint Chiefs of Staff, Senate Foreign Relations Committee, Aug. 15, 1963.
2. Ibid.
3. *U. S. News & World Report,* Jan. 27, 1964, p. 45.
4. Testimony of Dr. Edward Teller to Senate Preparedness Investigating Committee, Aug. 12, 1963.
5. *Collected Works of Lenin,* vol. 9, pp. 290-291; Proletarian No. 20, 1905.

Chapter 10: The Public is Too Dumb to Understand

1. Jordan, George R., *From Major Jordan's Diaries*, Bookmailer.
2. U. S. House Katyn Forest Committee, *Final Report*, Dec. 22, 1952.
3. Wedemeyer, General Albert C., *Wedemeyer Reports*, Holt.
4. Roswell L. Gilpatric, Deputy Secretary of Defense for 3 years in the Kennedy-Johnson Administration, *Foreign Affairs*, Apr. 1964, p. 368.
5. Senate Armed Services Committee, Hearings, Part 7, June 1962.
6. American Security Council, *Washington Report*, "Strategic Consequences of the Fulbright Memorandum," Oct. 11, 1961, pp. 1-8.
7. *Chicago Tribune*, June 18, 1962.
8. June 19, 1962, pp. 9966-8.
9. *Chicago Tribune*, Aug. 23, 1964.
10. *Human Events*, Mar. 17, 1962.
11. Reprint from Church League of America, Wheaton, Ill.
12. American Security Council, *Washington Report*, "Towards Convergence with Russia?" Feb. 3, 1964.
13. *The United States in the World Arena*.
14. ARPA-IDA Study Memo No. 7, Mar. 10, 1962, State Dept. Contract SCC 28270, Feb. 24, 1961.
15. Harriman, Averell, *Peace With Russia*, p. 2.

Chapter 11: Who's Lying Now?

1. Speech in Springfield, Ill., Aug. 19, 1964.
2. *New York Times*, Aug. 21, 1964.
3. *The Nation's Safety and Arms Control*, by Arthur T. Hadley, The Viking Press; a more technical statement of the same formula appears in

On Thermonuclear War, by Herman Kahn, Princeton Univ. Press.

4. *On Thermonuclear War,* p. 244.

5. *U. S. News & World Report,* Aug. 5, 1963, p. 39; these figures are substantially the same as the less complete tables contained in the release by Senator Goldwater dated from Springfield, Ill., Aug. 19, 1964, reported in the *New York Times,* Aug. 20, 1964, and generally confirmed in *Time,* Aug. 21, as "having some basis in fact — as far as it went," and in *Newsweek,* Aug. 24, 1964, as "right" on the "strict issue of arithmetic."

6. *Newsweek,* Aug. 24, 1964, p. 21.

7. See Chapter 6 on the Nitze Proposal.

8. Discussed in Chapter 7.

9. *U. S. News & World Report,* Oct. 21, 1963, p. 66: "General Power maintains that 'the B-47 in the hands of professionals, could deliver weapons in the year 2000'." "The entire fleet will be sent to a $3.5 billion scrap pile."

10. *Foreign Affairs,* April 1964. McNamara's endorsement was included in a Department of Defense Press Release reporting questions and answers on the occasion of an address by Mc-Namara to the Advertising Council, May 6, 1964.

Chapter 12: McNamara's Mono-Mega-Mania

1. Address to the United Nations, Sept. 26, 1961.

2. *"The Nation's Safety and Arms Control,"* by Arthur T. Hadley, The Viking Press, a book endorsed by Dr. Robert Oppenheimer, Dean Acheson and Professor Thomas C. Schelling.

3. Loss of U. S. technological superiority was first admitted 2 years after the event, in the testimony of the Joint Chiefs of Staff before the Senate

Committees in the Moscow Treaty hearings; reported in *U. S. News & World Report*, Aug. 26, 1963. Only one article revealing the incredible Soviet gains over the U. S. through the trap of Test-Ban I escaped the rigorous "unofficial" censorship and pressures employed to prevent the public from securing knowledge of what we had really lost. From *Life*, dated Feb. 16, 1962, it can be deduced that the Soviets increased their yield/weight ratio in high yield weapons by a factor of 5 to 10. The recent American Security Council's study entitled "Peace *and* Freedom," prepared by its National Strategy Committee, credits the Soviets with having increased, since 1960, "Their missile yield by a factor of 10 to 20, and their bomb yield by an even larger factor."

4. Confirmed in the testimony of the Joint Chiefs of Staff cited in footnote 3, *supra;* and see the statement in the *Interim Report by the Preparedness Investigating Subcommittee*, "Military Implications of the proposed limited Nuclear Test Ban Treaty," datd. Sept. 9, 1963, and substantially suppressed by the liberal press.

5. *Aviation Week & Space Technology*, March 16, 1964, p. 143.

6. Hearings on Defense Appropriations, Fiscal 1965, Part 5, pp. 57, 60.

7. *"Overkill Sophistry,"* by Dr. Stefan T. Possony, American Security Council Washington Report, June 17, 1963.

8. *Time*, Dec. 15, 1961.

9. *Aviation Week & Space Technology*, Mar. 16, 1964 rates Soviet missile payload as "probably . . . 35,000 lb.," and the largest U. S. missile, Titan II, at 7,000 lb., and Minuteman at 2,000 lb.

Chapter 13: A Nuclear Pearl Harbor?

1. Clark, Dr. Colin, *The Real Productivity of Soviet Russia,* Senate Internal Security Subcommittee, 1961.
2. House Un-American Activities Committee, Hearings, Sept. 14, 1960, p. 1911.
3. *U. S. News & World Report,* Apr. 8, 1963.
4. *Dark Side of the Moon,* Faber, London; U. S. House Select Committee on Communist Aggression, Second Report, Aug. 9, 1954.
5. Khrushchev's actual plan for world conquest, concealed by Aesopian language, is contained in his speech on "New Victories for the World Communist Movement," *World Marxist Review,* Jan. 1961. An analysis of this plan with documentation is contained in "New Myths and Old Realities of Nuclear War" by R. Adm. Chester Ward, (Ret.), *Orbis,* Fall 1964.
6. Senator Alben Barkley, Majority Leader.
7. *New York Times,* Feb. 12, 1945, *Time,* Feb. 19, 1945, *Life,* Feb. 26, 1945.
8. AP Dispatch, London, Aug. 15, 1964.
9. UPI Dispatch, Moscow, July 14, 1964.
10. *Washington Post,* July 6, 1960.

Chapter 14: Our Choice With No Second Chance

1. Johnson did not say the use of small nuclear tactical weapons "might" lead to escalation, but that "it *would* lead us down the uncertain path of blows and counterblows." *U. S. News & World Report,* Sept. 21, 1964, p. 116.
2. *Standard Research Journal,* Fourth Quarter, 1959, p. 124.
3. Daniel, James and Hubbell, John G., *Strike in the West.*

------ Cut Out and Mail ------

ORDER FORM

Pere Marquette Press,
P. O. Box 316, Alton, Illinois.

Send me _____ copies of THE GRAVEDIGGERS.

Payment of $_____ is enclosed (send check or money order).

Name_____

Street_____

City and State_____

(Please Print)

THE ISSUE
IS
SURVIVAL!

GIVE

THE GRAVEDIGGERS

To Friends and Neighbors. Ask doctors to give this
book to their patients, employers to give it to their
employees, parents to give it to college and high school
students, interested citizens to distribute it door-to-
door in their precinct or neighborhood. Give it to
opinionmakers such as editors, clergymen, teachers,
writers, and elected officials. Give it to members of
your church, club, union or fraternity. Distribute it
at meetings, on trains, in motels. Ask your local news-
stands, bookstores and libraries to carry it.

Do your part in this educational effort while there is
still time to . . .

KEEP THE PEACE
by
KEEPING AMERICA STRONG

QUANTITY PRICES

1 copy: $.75	10 copies: $5	100 copies: $30
3 copies: $2	25 copies: $10	500 copies: $125

1,000 or more copies $.20 each

*Illinois residents add 4% sales tax

PERE MARQUETTE PRESS
P. O. BOX 316   ALTON, ILLINOIS